Repairing the Ruins

Repairing the Ruins

The Classical and Christian Challenge to Modern Education

Canon Press

MOSCOW, IDAHO

Douglas J. Wilson, ed., *Repairing the Ruins: The Classical and Christian Challenge to Modern Education*

Published by Canon Press, P.O. Box 8741, Moscow, ID 83843.
800-488-2034

99 98 97 96   9 8 7 6 5 4 3 2 1

Cover design by Paige Atwood Design, Moscow, ID

Printed in the United States of America.

ISBN: 1-885767-14-5

Repairing the Ruins: The Classical and Christian Challenge to Modern Education

Introduction

Marlin Detweiler

Outside of the Gospel itself, nothing, and I do mean nothing, has affected my life more profoundly than the ramifications of discovering Christian classical education. I will not be surprised to learn that you may now or may soon come to share this same experience. Methodologically solid and biblically accountable Christian classical education is very much the order of the day.

To an historian, the recent resurgence of classical methodology in education is no surprise. When Johnny can't read, 'rite or do his 'rithmetic but feels good about it, someone is bound to notice and go looking for an alternative. Thankfully, God has graciously provided us with a written historical record of a time-proven method in the Trivium.

Dorothy Sayers, a mid 20th century writer and medieval historian, lamented the fact that this threefold method of teaching the grammar, dialectic and then rhetoric of any discipline had been virtually abandoned. And no wonder. The scholarly work of the Renaissance and Reformation is quite unmatched in our day. Why? Because we simply do not think well. We have not been taught to think. Today, proponents of the Trivium are once again seeing their children blossom in ways they never thought possible by applying this instructional system to the education of their children.

Who is to blame for where education is today? I am. You

are. I had four children before it even occurred to me that my responsibility to educate these gifts from God extended beyond choosing the school they would attend. The education of our children has been entrusted to someone or something else for far to long. Deuteronomy 6 makes quite clear what the parent's role is in educating their children. While I am entrusted with the care of my children, nothing I do is more important than bringing them up in the Lord. One can change careers every ten years, change ministry involvements whenever desirable, move from one location to another, but a parent has just one opportunity to raise his children. Wisdom lives in the cliche that no one ever says on his death bed "I should have spent more time at the office."

But, some will say, "We have many Christian schools, why do we need more?" A close examination of most Christian schools will lead to the conclusion that not only have we not educated the children well from the world's perspective (using an educational benchmark of at least a hundred years ago), we have not excelled at training young men and women to be godly either. A Christian school is not simply a government school with a Bible class added. It was once understood that Theology was the Queen of the Sciences. As spokes extend from the hub of a wheel so all disciplines tie together in God Himself. When we say Christian school we should mean sound biblical teaching in and for all of life. To love God with all our heart, soul, mind and strength and to love our neighbor as ourselves is what Christ taught as the greatest commandments. Disciplining our minds, our brains, according to God's Word is not as simple as memorizing Bible verses. Applying Scripture to all of life is no simple task. Rigorous study has always preceded Christian maturity. Jonathan Edwards, arguably the greatest pastor and philosopher to have been born in America, was known to study and pray thirteen hours a day, every day. The neatly packaged, get it at the convenience store, add Christ to your life type of Christianity is not biblical Christianity. Christian maturity never results from conversion alone.

Thankfully, today, many parents are waking up to the responsibility, blessing and opportunity of raising godly children.

This book is an ordered summary of talks given at national conferences of the Association of Classical and Christian Schools. They are moving. I trust you will be changed by having read them. I hope that you will be challenged to consider starting a Christian classical school or finding one for your children to attend. We are fortunate to have the relatively recent experiences of these men as resources to use in developing and applying the Christian classical educational model in our respective settings. It is quite likely that you will have no more timely and important opportunity in your entire life than to assist in the awesome task of "repairing the ruins."

Section One:

The Scriptural Worldview

ONE:

Introduction to Antithesis in Education
Douglas Wilson

The phrase *worldview Christianity* is capable of producing quite a comfortable glow, especially when used frequently in conversations with other Christians. But what does it mean?

When we undertake the task of relating the biblical faith to the world around us (which really is what Christian education *is*), we are confronted with at least four different relationships between our faith and the great wide world. Obviously, only one of the four relationships can be that taught by Scripture itself, but the other three have had, over the years, many well-meaning advocates within the Christian faith.

We may attempt to divorce the two. Tertullian asked, "What does Jerusalem have to do with Athens?" The pattern which produces this reaction is a familiar one. In a compromised age, many find it easy to react to the general compromise by running in what they think is the other direction. Because many of the early church fathers attempted to bring Jerusalem into subjection to Athens, Tertullian reacted by saying they had nothing to do with one another. This reaction has been repeated countless times since. In this, modern fundamentalists show their basic affinity with the monastic movements of early Catholicism. In Scripture, worldliness is an attitude; in all such mystic pietism, worldliness is in the

stuff—gotta stay away from the stuff. This is the pattern followed by all reactionary Christian academies—schools popu-
lated by refugees from condoms, knife fights, drug deals, ra-
cial tension, overtly atheistic teaching, *etc.* But a reaction
against the world is not the same thing as a positive biblical
vision for education.

For the second option, we may add our faith to the body
of knowledge we acquired elsewhere—added on as sort of a
condiment. Autonomous knowledge is a gray, pasty oatmeal,
available to everyone, while each person's religion of choice
provides the catsup, mustard, sugar, whatever works for them
in their own personal space. This is the view taken by many
Christian parents of kids in the government schools. The
school is supposed to teach all the "neutral subjects," and the
parents add the flavoring at home. But of course, neutrality is
impossible. And, as more and more parents have been discovering recently, somebody has been lacing this neutral
oatmeal, for a century or so, with the Cocaine of Rank Unbelief. The modern evangelical world has the theological acu-
men of a pile of wet sponges, but even we are starting to
catch on that something is amiss. "Hey!" we argue.

Some Christian schools take this same basic approach by
using the same fundamental curriculum as do the government
schools, but then adding prayer, a Bible class, or chapel. Christian education is seen as distinct because of the addition of a
new planet to the preexistent solar system of knowledge. But
true Christian education is a Copernican revolution which
comes to see Scripture as the sun at the center. And that sun,
that light, provides the light in which we see everything else.
Without that sun, we do not have objectivity; we have darkness.

Third, we may dilute our biblical convictions, but keep
the biblical terminology. The result is that we can detect a
pale taste of the faith everywhere. With this approach, the
faith and the world certainly interact, but if it were a wres-
tling match, the world would be sitting on the faith's head.

This approach is sometimes difficult to identify, but one help-ful rule of thumb would be to suspect any Christian school where dialogue is used as a verb. In the old days, Christians used to preach to Muslims, Hindus, Catholics, Mormons, *et al.* Now we are supposed to dialogue with them. Christians who "dialogue" with those of other faiths are using their faith as a branch upon which to perch lightly while they survey and appreciate all the other options. In schools governed by this approach, Christianity is a perspective; it is not the truth. This tendency is seen more often in those Christian schools which were founded more than a generation ago. The school carries on in the tradition of (insert name of denomination), but no one really believes it anymore.

The fourth option, that of the genuine biblical world-view, is to establish Scripture at every point as the founda-tion on which to build all knowledge. Moreover, Scripture is known to be the final arbiter of whether such knowledge was built in line with the foundation. If Jesus Christ is not the Lord of all, then two added to two does not equal four. If He did not die for the sins of His people, then A and ~ A cannot be distinguished. If the triune God of Scripture did not speak the universe into existence, then there is no uni-verse to understand. The protest will come—"But you are presupposing the truth of Christianity." And the answer which must follow is, "Most certainly. This is a Christian school." Those involved with a genuinely Christian school must understand the *antithesis* between faith and all forms of unbelieving thought at the very start of the process.

The Bible teaches that the fear of the Lord is the begin-ning of knowledge (Prov. 1:7). The fear of the Lord is not the final goal of education; such godly fear is the foundation of education, and as the foundation it is the basis for all subse-quent goals. We must remember that the label on the bottle does not dictate the contents of the bottle. A Christian school is not one which calls itself that, or even one in which all the occupants are regenerate people. A Christian school is one in which *the schooling itself* is being conducted in a biblical fashion.

This means that understanding of the biblical antithesis between belief and unbelief must be found throughout the curriculum. We must either think and educate like unbelievers, or we must think and teach as believers. This antithesis affects everything. "Christian teachers know that not a single 'fact' can really be known and therefore really be taught unless placed under the light of the revelation of God. Even the laws of arithmetic cannot be known otherwise."[1]

Of all these options, only one recognizes an antithesis between faith and unbelief which necessitates constant war between them. Every other option involves either peace through separation, or peace through compromise. But antithetical education sees that biblical instruction is not really taking place unless every thought is being made captive to the Lord Jesus Christ (2 Cor. 10:4). We cannot make peace with the world by running away from it, or by capitulating to it. J. Gresham Machen stated it this way: "The Christian cannot be satisfied so long as any human activity is either opposed to Christianity or out of all connection with Christianity. Christianity must pervade not merely all nations, but also all of human thought."[2]

True education must therefore be unabashedly Christian. The modern opium dream that education can be religiously neutral should be, in our minds, equivalent to the question of whether or not, to use a phrase found in Dabney's great essay, "schoolrooms should be located under water or in dark caverns."[3] Neutrality about the ultimate questions can be pretended in education, but it cannot be accomplished. There-

---

[1] Cornelius Van Til, *Foundations of Christian Education* (Phillipsburg, NJ: Presbyterian & Reformed Publishing Co.), p. 4.

[2] J. Gresham Machen, *Education, Christianity, and the State* (Jefferson, MD: The Trinity Foundation, 1987), p. 50.

[3] R.L. Dabney, *On Secular Education* (Moscow, ID: Canon Press, 1993), p. 12.

fore, all schools must confess that Jesus Christ is Lord over all and in all.

Returning to our center, this means an education which is biblically *antithetical*. Without an understanding of this antithesis, we will find ourselves unable to understand anything obediently. The foundation for comprehending this antithesis is found through careful, systematic study of the Word of God. Theology is the integration point for all knowledge, and sound theology is the study of the triune God as He reveals Himself in Scripture. It must be strongly emphasized that classical and Christian schools are necessarily evangelical Christian schools. We must reject both the mind-numbing errors of theological liberalism, and the superficial inanities of a reactionary fundamentalism. It is very important that Christians realize that they do not have to choose between genuine learning and a love for Christ. The greatest commandment includes the requirement that we love the Lord our God with all our *brains*. The truth of God revealed in Christ is something we must *comprehend*.

The antithesis has been with our race from the very beginning. In Genesis, God promised constant hostility between the seed of the woman and the seed of the serpent, and we have had it. From the beginning, God has placed enmity between the two. Sometimes the war is hot, and at other times the war is subdued and harder to recognize. But until the resurrection, God's people are always involved in constant, total war.

If God is good, and He is, and evil exists, and it does, then antithetical thinking on the part of His followers becomes a constant necessity. In a relativistic culture, there will be consistent attempts to destroy the distinctions between white and black. As Isaiah said, "Woe to those who call evil good, and good evil; who put darkness for light and light for darkness; who put bitter for sweet and sweet for bitter!" (Is. 5:20). But all such defiant attempts begin with the blurring of the distinction between white and *off-white*. There are many areas where God's people need a good deal of training—a good deal of *education*—before they can make the distinctions which God wants them to make. "But solid food belongs to those who are of full age, that is, those who by reason of use have their senses exercised to discern both good and evil" (Heb. 5:14).

Our ethical understanding of the world around us will be a reflection of the character of the God we serve. The God of the Bible is good, and He is unchanging. Therefore, an ethic based upon His revealed character will be good, and constantly good. Moreover, because God is sovereign His goodness applies everywhere; it fills all the various corners of every human endeavor. No human activity escapes His authority. But man is twisted, and he tries to escape this truth. Because man is mutable, he changes constantly. Therefore, a humanistic ethic based upon his man's character will also be twisted, and twisted into new shapes constantly. We do not need any other explanation for all the fads which sweep through the halls of modern education. Like the foolish women Paul mentions, they are always learning and never coming to a knowledge of the truth.

Education is the process of learning to serve one's God, and to fight all idols. Ours is the God of truth, so we serve Him in submission to His truth, and by rebelling against all lies. All denials of this antithesis are therefore epistemological camouflage as those on the other side of the line pretend there is no line—for strategic purposes of their own. In a war, what better strategy to use than to convince your enemy that there is no war?

This is not to portray unbelievers as omnicompetent. The disintegrating secular mind is not hard to miss. The good news is that, while we are not winning the war for the mind, the non-Christians are sure losing it. The non-believing mind has come to the end of its tether, and is now starting to leap in any old direction. Relativism now rules the postmodern mind. But this resultant cultural nihilism is an attempt to be consistent—which is inconsistent. Which, of course, is consistent. The opportunities are tremendous for those educators who will proclaim, without apology, the Christian world and life view, at the center of which is the God who declares this antithesis. Put simply, will it be God's way or man's way? Non-Christians can't think in a straight line, and modern Christians won't. When will Christian educators learn that Christianity goes far beyond saying that there is a right and a wrong *somewhere*? This is moralism, not the biblical antithesis. The antithesis says that there is a right and wrong *everywhere*. For educators, this means each classroom, the hallways, the administration offices, the playground, and the parking lot.

The antithesis divides the biblical worldview from all others, and everyone has a worldview. So the real issue is not whether we acknowledge a worldview, but rather which worldview we will acknowledge. The question is not whether we will have a God, but rather which one? Refusal to acknowledge this does not lead to non-worldview thinking, it leads to confused worldview thinking. And from such confusion, Christians are not exempt. We all certainly know that Christians can do "non-Christian" acts—this is what happens whenever we sin. In the same way, Christians can think "non-Christian" thoughts. A Christian worldview, therefore, is *not* defined as a worldview which happens to be held by Christians, any more than a "Christian act" is to be understood as anything which a Christian does. A Christian act is one which God requires of Christians; a Christian thought is defined the same way. Our dependence upon His revelation of Himself and His creation in Scripture is total and complete.

This clearly relates to education and the life of the mind. The greatest commandment includes the clause that we should love the Lord our God with all our *minds*. Education is a central part of the process of learning to do this, or refusing to learn to do this. And here is the antithesis. As educators, we either will obey Him in this, or we will not.

Is Classicism a Denial of Antithesis?

This strong emphasis on antithesis may cause some readers to wonder about the compatibility of Christian education with classical education. Are not *classical* and *Christ-centered* themselves on opposite sides of this antithetical divide? So how can a school purport to be pursuing both? Why do we even want to try?

Christianity is not an abstraction. Christ was born in history, in Judea, in the reign of Caesar Augustus. In the providence of God, the Christian faith then spread north and west. The impact of the kingdom of God on the history of our culture has been monumental. While the kingdom of God cannot be *identified* with western culture (and we do not seek even to try), that kingdom nevertheless has had such an impact on the West that the history of either since the time of Christ is incomprehensible without detailed understanding of the history of the other.

This requires that we seek to provide an education grounded in the culture of the West. To resort to a commonplace, when parents teach their children to speak, the language they teach is the language they themselves speak. In other words, the young are always educated by *their* elders. God has placed us in this particular cultural river; our children have no ability to flow in a different stream.

This principle is recognized clearly when we are talking about parents and their children—just one generation. But it applies, just as clearly, when we take our grandparents and ancestors into account—all the way back to the birth of our Lord in the reign of Caesar Augustus, and before that to the covenant made with Abraham, and before that to the fall of our father Adam. Education cannot be successfully detached from our cultural river, and turned into a small private pond. If any such attempt is made, the result will be a poor cultural education, not a culturally neutral education.

This is not xenophobic, or an expression of any desire to react mindlessly to the modern trendiness of multiculturalism.

If this duty of cultural education is neglected, the result will not be appreciation for other cultures, but rather a poor training in one's own, and a resultant contempt for one's own. Cultural excellence in the education of our children is therefore not a side issue. The one best equipped to understand and appreciate another man's culture is the man who understands and appreciates his own.

Of course, for Christian educators the phrase *Christ-centered* must remain a constant. By it is meant the Christian faith and worldview, as it is set forth in the Scriptures, and only there. Those Scriptures teach what the world refers to as evangelical Protestantism, defined best in the historical confessions of the Reformation. Now of course there are competing definitions. Other faiths claim to be "Christ-centered," but a refutation of all such competing claims would take us far beyond the scope of this essay. For our purposes here, the doctrine referred to by *Christ-centered* is that of historic evangelical Christianity.

And this generates our question. Modernity does not have a high view of the intellectual horsepower of evangelicalism. Evangelical faith is thought to be a Bible-beating faith—no thought required. And so when evangelical Christians seek to provide a classical education, the question *what are they doing?* immediately presents itself. In the realm of education, the word *classical* can have three basic meanings. With the first two definitions, the word definitely represents a conflict with the Christian understanding of antithesis. But with the third definition, there is a perfect and necessary harmony.

The first definition of *classical* seeks to bypass the last two thousand years of history, and return to a study of the golden ages of Greece and Rome—Periclean Athens and Augustan Rome. This return may be very narrow in focus (linguistic studies in a classical studies department), or it may be as broad as a culture-wide attempt to return to the pagan classical world, *e.g.*, certain influential portions of the Renaissance. While this use of *classical* is certainly antithetical to the

Christian faith, it also does not today present much of a danger. While there is a great deal of neo-paganism in our culture today, it is not a civilized paganism. The barbarism that threatens to engulf our schools is neo-barbarism, and not the neo-paganism of an attempted Renaissance. Fifteen minutes watching heavy metal on MTV should remind educated viewers of barbarians at the gates; there is an obvious and vicious delight in tearing civilizations down. We are not confronted with the sophisticated unbelief of Julian the Apostate; the spectacle is rather one of America's postmodern whore Madonna, or the nihilistic destructiveness of a Kurt Cobain. Even though such barbarous activity has been seen for millennia, the word *classical* does not come to mind.

The second definition of *classical* is also rooted in antiquity but also takes the last two thousand years into account. The problem with it is that it is syncretistic, that is, the basic concepts, ideas, and philosophies of the classical world are combined (in various ways) with Christian theology—in a way that does violence to the integrity of Christian theology.

Probably the best example of this would be Aristotelian Thomism. Aristotle, of course, was the great Greek philosopher who taught in the fourth century, B.C.. Up until the 13th century, A.D. the efforts of most syncretists were Platonist, *i.e.*, they sought to express "Christian" truths in terms of Plato's philosophy. (There are still some holdouts here and there—*e.g.*, C.S. Lewis was very much under the influence—"It's all in Plato. Bless me, what do they teach them in these schools?") But in the 13th century the Catholic scholastic giant Thomas Aquinas took the radical step of resurrecting the philosophy of Aristotle, and expressing it with the vocabulary of a Christian. The resultant philosophy is called *Thomism*, and is very prevalent in the Roman Catholic church today—Thomas Aquinas is considered by that church as one of her "doctors." In the realm of classical education, we can see this influence today with men such as Mortimer Adler. When it comes to pedagogical philosophy, Mortimer Adler is an unapologetic Aristotelian. The philosophy of Aristotle is pervasive in his writings—at times explicit, and always present.

The central problem with this is that it requires a humanistic and autonomous approach to truth that is totally at odds with the biblical revelation of truth in Christ. For example, it is impossible to imagine a thinking Christian saying, as Adler did say, something like this—"Only the liberal arts can provide the standard for judging excellence in teaching, for measuring the efficiency of educational means, or for inventing others; and the liberal arts are neither pagan nor Christian, but human."[4] It is clear that any classicism like this is unacceptable for Christians because Christ is Lord of all.

But the third use of *classical* is thoroughly Christian, and grounded in the great truths of Scripture recovered and articulated at the Reformation. This classicism is an antithetical classicism, best illustrated by the relationship of the apostle Paul to the philosopher Aristotle and the learning of the classical world.

Paul was not unaware of Aristotelian philosophy. He had been well-educated under Gamaliel, and demonstrated in his writings a thorough knowledge of Greek philosophy and culture. He knew the language (Acts 21:37), he knew their poets (Acts 17:28), he quoted Diogenes the Cynic (1 Tim. 6:10), he knew their current philosophies (Acts 17:17), and he knew the thought of Aristotle. In short, Paul was well-trained in classical culture. But this did not gain him an entry into their circles. The only problem was that he was a classicist who would not play the game of autonomous and humanistic philosophers. He was a classicist who did not fit in well at the philosophy department at the University of Athens (Acts 17:18). They didn't think a lot of him, but then again, he was happy to return fire.

---

[4] Mortimer Adler, *Reforming Education* (New York, NY: Collier Books, 1990), p. 179.

Where is the wise? Where is the scribe? Where is the disputer of this age? Has not God made foolish the wisdom of
this world? For since, in the wisdom of God, the world
through wisdom did not know God, it pleased God through
the foolishness of the message preached to save those who
believe (1 Cor. 1:20-21).

But it is in the next chapter that he deals with Aristotle:

But the natural man does not receive the things of the Spirit
of God, for they are foolishness to him; nor can he know
them, because they are spiritually discerned (1 Cor. 2:14).

When modern Christians read the phrase *natural man*,
they tend to think of unregenerate man at his worst—the drug
addict, the philanderer, the alcoholic. But Paul is making an
entirely different point. He is talking about unregenerate man
at his best. The word *natural* here (*psychikos*) was a word that
was coined by Aristotle, and was used by him to refer to man
at the peak of his form—man the way he would look after he
had completed a rigorous and "classical" education. This is
the man who, according to Paul, does not know God, cannot
know God, and does not receive the things of the Spirit.

So we see in Paul a biblical classicist. He does not run
from classical culture, nor is he defeated or compromised by
it. Rather, he declares the lordship of Jesus Christ *over* it. He
does not run away, and he does not compromise. He takes
every thought captive to Jesus Christ. He uses his vast learning in the cause of the gospel (Acts 26:24), but had seen enough
secular scholarship to warn the church at Colossae to beware
of "philosophy and empty deceit" (Col. 2:8).

Human culture is to be despised by Christians only when
it seeks to function autonomously. When human culture seeks
to do what only the grace of God can do, then it is to be
vigorously opposed by thinking Christians. But when the
classical knee is bent to the lordship of Christ (note: not when
pagan and Christian terms, categories, *etc.* are merged and

confused), then, and only then, will a classical and Christian approach emerge—Christian because the Scripture is the final authority on all issues, and classical because the culture that has been redeemed in this submission is our western culture, along with all that made it what it is.

This kind of classical culture and education has been seen before—in the Protestant West from the time of the Reformation down through the middle of the nineteenth century. If God is gracious to us, and grants us repentance for what we have so carelessly thrown away, we may be granted a chance to rebuild. In doing this we are trying to establish an education system that equips Christian leaders. In the daunting task of cultural restoration, which is what we face, it is crucial that we train our children to continue the work we have begun. And this is truly antithetical education.

TWO:

The Importance of Personal Holiness
Douglas Wilson

A school must be built by men and women. No "sinner-proof" method has yet been discovered which will guarantee the success of any school, or secure the blessing of God upon it. Such things cannot be built by formula; a school which honors God cannot be purchased or used as a paint-by-numbers kit. This means a group of people intent on building a school can go to all the right conferences, read the right Christian books on education, embrace the classical vision, and still wind up with an atrocity for a school. When things go wrong in this world, as they frequently do, sin is at the heart of it. When God blesses, as He loves to do, holiness is at the heart of it.

Elsewhere in this book, it has been made plain that the classical Christian school movement is part of the historic Protestant faith. There is far more to this than a sectarian and partisan flag-waving, or a desire for ecclesiastical "roots." The apostle tells us that we are to live by faith from first to last (Rom. 1:17). This being the case, our understanding of *what faith means* is critical. We live in an age which is impatient with careful theological distinctions, and this is all the more reason why they must be made. We are justified by faith, and we walk by faith—we should know what that means. Martin Luther once commented that justification by faith was the article of a standing or falling church. In a very similar way,

it is the mark of a standing or falling Christian school. Without the gospel, a Christian school is nothing, and without a
proper understanding of justification, the gospel is nothing.
"For indeed the gospel was preached to us as well as to them;
but the word which they heard did not profit them, not being mixed with faith in those who heard it" (Heb. 4:2). Faith
is essential and consequently a proper understanding of faith
and justification by faith is essential.

This is not a vain quibbling over words. For example, a
well-known association of Christian schools requires all member schools to be evangelical Protestant schools, which is good.
At the same time, that association's statement of faith requires
those who sign to affirm an *anti*-Protestant understanding of
justification by faith. Whether this is the result of doctrinal
confusion, or represents something more sinister is not really
the point. The point is that the *name* Protestant does not
guarantee anything.

The objective reality of our justification is grounded upon
the righteousness of Jesus Christ. We are put right with God
because of *the goodness of somebody else*. Just as Adam's sin
was imputed to every man, in the same way, Christ's righteousness was imputed to every saved man. The ground of
this justification is the righteousness of Jesus Christ, while
the instrument for receiving it is our faith. It cannot be emphasized too strongly that we are *not* justified on the basis of
our faith. We are justified on the basis of *Christ's* faith and
work. This gospel message of free grace liberates—it liberates
from the condemnation of sin once for all, and from the power
of sin progressively.

When men are put right with God by this message of free
justification, do they then begin to sin so that "grace may
abound"? As Paul would say, *no way*. God has never yet justified a man without setting him apart and beginning the long,
slow, painful process of sanctifying him. We must be careful
never to separate what God has joined together. Justification
and sanctification are distinct, but they are never separated.

They are not the same work, but the one who works in us for His good purposes always accomplishes both.

This is said by way of introduction. Whenever the standards of personal holiness and discipline are emphasized in a school (as they must be), the temptation will follow to forget grace, or at least deemphasize it. But both must be remembered and emphasized, each in its proper place. The centrality of Christ's righteousness is imputed to us by faith alone, and this provides the only possible foundation for righteous Christian living. Because the rest of this essay is directed at certain standards of personal conduct in a Christian school, I thought it was important to acknowledge the only possible foundation for this personal conduct. Paul has a good deal to say about personal holiness in the last three chapters of Ephesians. But he builds his exhortations on the doctrinal foundation he laid in the first three chapters. Who we are in Christ is the only foundation for what we do in the imitation of Christ.

When the foundation of Christ's righteousness is understood, visible personal holiness in a Christian school is extremely important.[†] We are not to set the standards low. Those who work in a Christian school are in a *de facto* leadership position in the Christian community. We must therefore understand the difference between the qualifications for *leadership* and the qualifications for *fellowship*. If someone has confessed his sin and the lordship of Christ, then we should be fully prepared to fellowship together with him. But responsibility for others means that God sets and requires a higher standard. For example, the qualifications for elders in a church are not the same as qualifications for members in

---

[†] The standards apply to anyone in a position of authority in the school. Among Logos School's six foundational goals is this one: "Provide a clear model of biblical Christian life through the school staff and board (Matthew 22:37-40)." *Logos School Policy Manual* 2.3.

the church. No one connected with a Christian school should chafe at this higher standard. To whom much is given, much is required. Teaching is an honored profession, as it ought to be. The standards should therefore be high. If the Christian school doesn't respect teaching enough to protect its reputation through discipline, then how can we expect others to respect what *we* despise?

At the same time, without lowering God's standards, we must be realistic. We must understand that everyone connected with the school is involved in the battle against sin, and there will be times when they stumble. Take the example of two homes with multiple children, one home clean and the other trashed. The difference between them is not how many things are dropped, spilled, dirtied, *etc.* The difference between them is how many things are picked up, cleaned, *etc.* When students or parents are sinned against, that sin does not go away all by itself. It must be addressed, and addressed clearly. A Christian school therefore must be filled with board members, administrators, and teachers *who apologize.* For example, if a teacher was visibly impatient with a class, then that teacher should apologize to that class. This will not diminish their respect for this teacher—quite the reverse. If an administrator failed to notify a parent about something when he promised to do so, then he should apologize, not excuse.

As we set ourselves to deal with sin, we must comprehend the importance of the intangibles. True holiness involves far more than staying away from your neighbor's wife and refusing to rob filling stations. Holiness involves more than staying away from gross sin, and it involves something other than following a list of detailed rules of our own devising. The rules are God's laws, not man's. When they are obeyed with a true heart, the obedience results in a pervasive aroma— the aroma of spiritual bread baking. "For we are to God the fragrance of Christ among those who are being saved and among those who are perishing. To the one we are the aroma of death leading to death, and to the other the aroma of life leading to life. And who is sufficient for these things?" (2 Cor. 2:15-16). For those who love God, an aroma like this which is pervasive in the school will make the school a *pleasant* place to be.

In the process of sanctification, the practice of holiness teaches us much. "But solid food belongs to those who are of full age, that is, those who *by reason of use* have their senses exercised to discern both good and evil" (Heb. 5:14). Virtually all Christians understand that certain "big" sins are to be avoided. But your Christian school should not be satisfied with avoidance of the big sins—you should take care that the nuances of godly living are understood and practiced. As the author of Hebrews says, our senses should be *exercised* to make such fine distinctions. Just because you can see the big E on the eye chart does *not* mean you do not need glasses.

Standard Temptations

Of course, all board members, administrators, and teachers must combat the standard temptations which come to all those who are breathing. Whether they are temptations involving money, sex, or difficult family relations, those involved in Christian education have received no special exemption from such trials. With all Christians everywhere, we must, as pilgrims and sojourners, "abstain from fleshly lusts which war against the soul" (1 Pet. 2:11). As those in a position of leadership, of course the staff of a Christian school should not be defeated by such temptations. At the same time, leadership does not mean an ability to walk two inches above the ground.

However, some temptations do come with the territory— or at least the *form* of the temptation is clearly affected by the school environment. When sin is a problem in a Christian school, the name of God is reviled in a way that does not happen in the most secular government school. A Christian school which tolerates hypocrisy is training the students in ungodliness. An ungodly Christian school is far worse than an ungodly government school. "For 'the name of God is blasphemed among the Gentiles because of you,' as it is written" (Rom. 2:24). Parents have no business putting their children in *either*. The short discussion below will only briefly address some of the more common problems with sin in Christian schools. But the brevity of the discussion in no way reflects the importance of the various issues.

At the board and administrative level, there will be many opportunities to *compromise*. The motives to compromise will be many—cowardice, desire for financial viability, man-pleasing, *etc.*—and the opportunities to compromise will be varied—a board member's son who is a discipline problem, discipline of a staff member which would embarrass the school, *etc.* But the compromise itself is a much greater threat to the school than the danger you are trying to avoid through the compromise.

Another common problem area is with *authority*—a problem doing what your superiors instructed you to do, and doing it the way they wanted it done. "Bondservants, obey in all things your masters according to the flesh, *not with eyeservice, as menpleasers*, but in sincerity of heart, fearing *God*. And whatever you do, do it heartily, as to the Lord and not to men, knowing that from the Lord you will receive the reward of the inheritance; for you serve the Lord Christ. But he who does wrong will be repaid for what he has done, and there is no partiality" (Col. 3:22-25). This requirement was placed on Christian slaves in the first century. The requirement was not weakened when the master was a fellow-believer; rather it was strengthened. "And those who have believing masters, let them not despise them because they are brethren, but rather serve them because those who are benefited are believers and beloved. Teach and exhort these things" (1 Tim. 6:2). This is certainly a place where we may argue *a fortiori*. If a Christian *slave* was to work diligently for a Christian master, how much more should Christian teachers do the same and more for the schools which employ them?

Of course, Christians will often do what they are told,

but with a good deal of grumbling. But the Scriptures prohibit this as well. "Do all things *without complaining and disputing*, that you may become blameless and harmless, children of God without fault in the midst of a crooked and perverse generation, among whom you shine as lights in the world . . ." (Phil. 2:14-15). Often a school will say, in glossy promotional material, that it wants to present a true alternative to the world's way of doing things. The Bible tells us that one clear way to do this is to abstain from grumbling. A refusal to complain is true alternative education. And grumbling in the halls of a Christian school is not an alternative; it is just another wind instrument in that great secular orchestra of whiners. The occasion for grumbling does not really matter. Scripture does not say to refuse a complaining spirit unless it involves the superintendent's decision to prohibit coffee for teachers in the classroom. Or the unfair rotation schedule of lunch duty.

This is related to another temptation, which is that of impatience. One clear characteristic of a good teacher is *patience*. Just trying to *explain* a writing assignment to seventh graders is enough to send some people around the bend. "Can I put my name in the space *above* the top line?" "Is a mechanical pencil all right? I lost my other one." Anger and impatience are common stumbling blocks for inexperienced teachers. The cause of this is *another* sin, which is inadequate discipline. When a teacher wants to be accepted or liked, he does not put a disciplinary system in place while the kids are behaving. While they are behaving, he is qualified to do so, but he does not feel like it. When they get to misbehaving, as they will, he is now motivated to discipline, but is not spiritually qualified to do so. "Brethren, if a man is overtaken in any trespass, *you who are spiritual* restore such a one in a spirit of gentleness, considering yourself lest you also be tempted" (Gal. 6:1). Because he tries to discipline when he is spiritually unqualified, the result is impatience and anger. Discipline should always be judicial and *calm*. Moreover, discipline should be strict and painful. If it is not painful, it is not discipline. "Now no chastening seems to be joyful for the present, *but painful*; nevertheless, afterward it yields the peaceable fruit of righteousness to those who have been trained by it" (Heb. 12:11). Because true discipline is painful to the students, a kindhearted teacher will often avoid it until the time when the discipline can only be administered in an ungodly, exasperated manner.

Another temptation is *laziness*. When a teacher is first hired, laziness is difficult because so many preparations have to be made for each new class. But once the teacher has been teaching the same courses for a number of years, it is perilously easy to get stuck in a groove. Associated with this is the temptation to get on a high horse when this possibility is even brought up. "I'm a professional, and I am insulted when . . ." Of course the teaching profession is incredibly demanding—*when approached properly*. But it can also be seen as an indoor job with no heavy lifting, and has been used that way by many. The answer to this is accountability. When teachers are required to have lesson plans in every Friday, they should not take it as a personal insult. "Doesn't the administration trust us?" The short answer is no—but no godly Christian trusts *himself* either. We need accountability and the encouragement of discipline. A godly Christian is not someone who does not need external discipline and accountability. A godly Christian is one who responds cheerfully and humbly to such external discipline. This applies at every level of authority—from the board to the administration, from the administration to the staff, and from the teachers to the students.

As a last consideration, administrators and teachers also need to recognize the governmental boundaries which God has established. We may sin through an instrusive "doing good." When God has required someone to meet a particular need, and for various reasons, he is not doing so, this does not mean that others are automatically authorized to step into his place. The two principal governments requiring such recognition are those of family, where teachers are frequently tempted to step over the line in ministering to kids, and that of marriage, where administrators are tempted to forget dad and just deal with mom. (For more on this, see Tom Spencer's chapter on *In Loco Parentis.*)

We cannot expect Christian students to think and behave like Christian students when we are not thinking and behaving like Christian educators. And the heart of thinking like a Christian, in any area, is the recognition that devotion to Christ is not optional. Some worldview educators, in seeing that the individuality and subjectivism of *pietism* has had a truly destructive impact on Christian culture, have adopted the additional and mistaken belief that *personal piety* is also to be rejected. On the contrary, personal piety is the only possible starting point for all our endeavors.

THREE:

Godly Discipline and the Christian School
Tom Spencer

I have worked at Logos School for the past eleven years. Five years ago, I became the first secondary principal at Logos School. This background reveals some of my perspective on discipline. Most of my experience involves working with junior-high and high-school students. My wife and I have been blessed with four children of our own. (All boys, however; young girls remain somewhat of a mystery to me.)

I never aspired to be a Christian school administrator. Initially I did not have a vision for this job. Why would anyone willingly choose to be a principal? What a dumb job! All I saw were the problems of dealing with unhappy parents and having to enforce student discipline. What fun! I see the role much differently now. One of the most significant changes that has occurred is my understanding of the opportunity inherent in every disciplinary situation to teach and to disciple students. Nearly every time you speak to a student regarding discipline, you have the opportunity to remind the student of God's standard for our behavior. We hope that reminding students of God's standards will result in the students confessing sin and repenting, according to God's grace. In the same way, non-Christian students may come to realize again the impossibility of being able to achieve God's standard for righteousness apart from the saving grace of our Lord Jesus Christ.

Disciplining students is teaching students. Godly discipline teaches *all* of the students in your school about God. Effective discipline continually brings students back to what God has said in His word, to what He has identified as right, and to what He has declared to be sin. This of course is not a dumb job at all, but a tremendous opportunity to love and encourage children toward righteous behavior.

This short essay is not sufficient to address the primary building block of your school's discipline practices. To be able to discipline students effectively, teachers and administrators must have a working knowledge of God's Word as it relates to the topic of discipline. This chapter is really a specific application of the previous chapter on personal holiness.

For example, one passage of Scripture that has influenced my philosophy of discipline is Ephesians 3:14-15, "For this reason, I kneel before the Father, from whom all fatherhood in heaven and on earth derives its name." As I fulfill the role of father to my children, I am to look to God the Father for my example. I am to look to Him to see how He loved His Son. I look to him to see how He disciplined His people. So often children (wrongly, but understandably) project the attributes of their own father on to their personal understanding of God's character. If I do my job well, my children will be better able to understand God's character, and His love for them as children adopted into His family. As a school, we understand the idea of *in loco parentis* (in place of the parents). During the school day, we are serving temporarily in the place of the parents. So, this Scripture applies to us well.

How does God discipline? Proverbs 3:12 says that "the Lord disciplines those He loves, as a father disciplines the son He delights in." Our motivation for discipline clearly must be love for and delight in the child. This is a part of God's example to us as our Father.

School personnel must understand the biblical concepts of love, justice, forgiveness, restitution, mercy, swift and painful discipline, *etc.* They must understand the nature of chil-

dren and why children need discipline. Teachers must also
understand the difference between rules based on God's Word
and rules based on personal preferences and/or culture. Some
have called this second type of rules "house rules."[1]

Your admissions process and your discipline needs are
directly related whether you realize it or not. The amount
and kind of discipline that your school will enforce each day
is directly related to your adopted mission statement. What
type of school are you going to be? Are you seeking to be
primarily an evangelistic school working with a majority of
non-Christian students? Or are you planning to work with
Christian students raised in homes by Christian parents?
Shortly after Logos School was founded, a Christian school
consultant strongly encouraged the school board and administration not to try to be both. This was wise counsel. Despite your decision, you should think through how your discipline policies relate to your school's mission statement. Your
admissions standards and your discipline policies should be
integrated. As a school that has a mission to encourage Christian students, we generally will not admit students who have
records of misconduct at a government school. Paul warned
the church at Corinth that, "Don't you know, a little yeast
works though the whole batch of dough" (1 Cor. 5:6). We
have seen this truth lived out in practice. Think twice before
you admit the "yeast" into your school. We have witnessed
the negative impact one sour attitude can have on an entire
class, even if most of the students in the class are Christians.

---

[1] One book that has been a very practical help to me in developing a biblical philosophy of discipline is Bruce A. Ray's book,
Withhold Not Correction. At Logos our new staff members, especially those who do not have children, are required to read this
book as part of their orientation process. It helps them to learn and
understand a biblical basis and philosophy of discipline. Douglas
Wilson also has a tape series on *Biblical Childrearing* available from
Canon Press. The book of Proverbs is of course full of information
about discipline.

We have also witnessed the blessings that follow from removing these individuals from the school. The entire spirit
of the class will change as a result. We have also learned that
it is better to avoid enrolling misbehaving students in the first
place. As a private school, you are under no compulsion to
admit every student who applies for admission to your school.
Your admissions decisions are important ones. When deciding, you must weigh the benefits to the individual student
against the impact on the entire class. The admissions decision is a very important decision.

A successful discipline program is made up of several component parts. First, the school board must establish certain
policies related to discipline.[2] Second, administrators should
establish guidelines to help the staff implement these policies. Guidelines are also necessary to address areas that the
policies do not cover. Finally, the teachers themselves must
establish rules for their own classrooms. Working together
to coordinate certain rules is important for both elementary
and secondary teachers.

Your school board *must* create discipline policies. These
policies should identify, to the students and to the parents,
the particular offenses that the school board considers as especially serious. Examples are disrespect or defiance shown
toward a teacher, or physical fighting, or the use of obscene
language. Policies should address the situation of a student
who displays a continuing pattern of misbehavior. The matter of corporal punishment must be considered. The board
should also establish a process by which students may be sus-
pended or expelled.

As previously mentioned, the administrators must develop
guidelines that give the staff direction for carrying out the
board's policies. For example, if sending students to the office is an option available to the teachers, it should be clear

---

[2] Sample discipline policies are available from Logos School,
110 Baker Street, Moscow, ID, 83843.

when they should do so. Who decides what discipline will be meted out, the administrator or the teacher? Who is responsible for contacting the parents? If you have a dress code, how are dress code violations dealt with? Suffice it to say that the administrator should clearly define roles. At the secondary level, students may have four or five different teachers every day. For the sake of the students, class rules among these teachers should be coordinated as much as possible. The administrator should take the lead in seeing that this is done.

Teachers will address most of the day-to-day discipline in the classroom. The administrator should help the classroom teachers in developing their class rules. This is especially true for new teachers. In fact, it may be best if the administrator provides the classroom teachers with a draft of classroom rules that are appropriate. They can then discuss modifications to make the rules fit the style and needs of the individual teacher. Overall, fewer rules are better than a laundry list of offenses. The most critical component of classroom discipline is that teachers *consistently* enforce classroom rules. One of the easiest ways for a teacher to lose the respect of his students is to appear arbitrary and capricious when it comes to the enforcement of discipline.

The willingness and ability to enforce discipline is one chief advantage of hiring teachers who are good parents. New teachers naturally want students to like them. They are often afraid that if they discipline a student, the student will dislike or even hate them. Teachers learn by experience that the opposite is true, students will respect teachers who enforce discipline consistently. Teachers who are already parents do not seem to have the same hesitancy when it comes to enforcing discipline. Administrators should spend extra time helping teachers who do not have children to address this need. Last year, the Logos student council helped to create a survey instrument designed to give the teachers feedback from the students. The standards they included were insightful. The way a teacher managed his classroom was obviously very important to the students. The students included questions like, "Is class time used productively?", "Does the teacher discipline without emotion?", and "Are the discipline standards appropriate to the activity?" on the survey they constructed. Teachers must manage their classrooms effectively to be successful teachers.

In all matters of discipline, pray for wisdom and discernment. "If any of you lacks wisdom, he should ask God, who gives generously to all without finding fault, and it will be given to him" (Jas. 1:5). "For the Lord gives wisdom, and from his mouth come knowledge and understanding" (Prov. 2:6). Often I have longed for the book titled, *How to judge righteously in each and every situation you will face as a school principal (or a teacher)*. However, it seems that each situation you face is a little bit different. Obviously there is not a step-by-step how-to book. Each situation and each student is different. So, we must pray. We need wisdom. We need to understand the character of the child with whom we are dealing. Guy Doud, 1988 teacher of the year, described literally sitting in the desks of his students asking God for discernment about their character. We must understand the character and personality of the students we discipline. Any teacher who has ever been assigned to supervise elementary recess knows firsthand our need for wisdom and discernment. (How about a 1-800-Sol-omon phone line?) We should also seek the counsel of other Christians. In reality, very few disciplinary situations require an immediate decision. While enforcing discipline swiftly is important, especially for young children, take the time to discuss the situation with other believers before making a decision.

To enforce discipline, we must also learn to be excellent listeners and to ask the right questions. "The first to present his case seems right, till another comes forward and questions him" (Prov. 18:17). Before making a judgment, be sure you have your facts straight. It is discouraging to discipline a student and *then* to receive a critical piece of information.

"Everyone should be quick to listen, slow to speak, and slow to become angry" (Jas. 1:19). Also, be certain to ask questions of each student involved.

Administrators should always support the discipline decision of the teachers in front of the students. Teachers should support administrators in the same fashion. Much like with a good marriage, the students or children should see a united front. If there is a problem, the individuals should discuss it in private. If a mistake was made, the teacher or administrator should go back later and ask forgiveness of the student.

Remember that discipline is teaching. The principal should not assume that his disciplinary decisions or discussions with an individual student will remain private. Plan on the fact that other students will ask the disciplined student, "what happened?" Act accordingly. If you know that God has declared a certain behavior to be wrong, you need to discipline a student to enforce and uphold this standard. You are not teaching one student, you are really teaching all of the students. There are times when you should go speak to an entire class for the sake of avoiding rumors or gossip, such as during a suspension or an expulsion. You may also want to pray for the student with the rest of the class.

At a workshop during our first ACCS teacher training week last summer, one participant asked Tom Garfield and me if we would share some mistakes that we had made. It was a good question, although an uncomfortable question to answer. Anyway, we can learn from our mistakes. Be careful to match the discipline given with the offense. One of my most painful, yet profitable, conferences was with a parent I highly respected. The parents shared that their daughter felt that a couple of my disciplinary decisions were not just. The reason was that the punishment seemed more severe that the offense. Upon reflection, the student was right. I had given a harsher sentence than the behavior deserved. Students have an innate, and strong, sense of justice. As an administrator, you must have the respect of the students and parents in your school.

Do not take students' misbehavior personally. Be consistent in your calls and sure that your decision matches the offense.

I admire Robert E. Lee very much for the manner in which he disciplined his officers. He was both firm and gentle when it came to having to discipline one of his officers. He provided discipline when necessary, yet clearly had the respect of his officers. He knew when to be strict and when to be merciful. As Shakespeare wrote, "The quality of mercy is not strained, It droppeth as the gentle rain from heaven upon the place beneath. It is twice blest; It blesseth him that gives and him that takes . . ."[3]

We must also be careful when responding to legalistic parents. Being a person who doesn't like telling parents *no*, in my early years I made decisions that always reduced activities to the lowest common denominator. We once had the junior-high students come to school in the evening for an American history dinner. During and after dinner, we played some music related to the colonial period in U.S. history. Some girls started to dance, some by themselves and others with girl partners. A couple of girls danced with their fathers. The next day I found myself facing two very stern faces in my office. These parents informed me that one reason that they had enrolled their children at Logos was to avoid dances, which they considered sinful. I listened to their concern. I do not recall if I offered an apology (I hope not). I did assure them that this would not happen again.

Later, the same student who pointed out my harsh sentence, let me know that she found my response troubling. I realized that by trying to prevent any activity that might offend a few, I was limiting the activities of the entire student body, although they were violating no biblical standard. The lesson is that you cannot please everyone. So, you have to be willing to make decisions based on principles you believe in, and accept the fact that some people will protest.

---

[3] William Shakespeare, *The Merchant of Venice.*

Our school is in an area with several local churches who have pastors that clearly teach God's Word. They practice church discipline when necessary. We are operating with an advantage that you may not have, namely, we have many parents who have been well taught about biblical discipline. Consequently, most of our parents support our discipline policies and decisions. The task for those in schools who do not have this support will be more challenging. I encourage you to stand firm in establishing and upholding God's standard of righteousness in your school. I would rather have a smaller school with parents who supported our philosophy than a large school without the support of the parents.

Keep discipline in perspective. Our task is education. Our goal is to create a productive learning environment in the classroom. Stay focused on the central task before us, the education of the students in our school. Yet discipline is a part of that process. Students in Christian schools need discipline. May God use this discipline to mold and shape their character to be more like Christ.

In writing this essay, I have thought about my qualifications to write a chapter on discipline. I am a sinner saved by God's grace. I have sinned in matters of discipline both as a parent and as an administrator. I have asked for forgiveness from my children and from students at Logos School. I know the richness of God's grace. I have not received what I deserve. I have been blessed by being able to sit under the teaching of gifted pastors, clearly equipped to teach God's Word. I hope that my experiences will somehow be a benefit and encouragement to you.

FOUR:

The Scriptural Worldview
Chris Schlect

I became aware of the necessity for sound, biblical thinking in each of the academic disciplines while I was in college. At that time I had become convinced from Scripture that up to that point in my academic career I had been disobedient to the greatest commandment: to love God with all of my heart, soul, and *mind*. I had no idea of what a distinctively Christian outlook on mathematics or history would be like, but I knew that as a student I was called to develop such an outlook.

My high school graduation ceremony capped twelve years of instruction in government schools. I had succeeded in my studies, I thought, having earned a strong G.P.A. and an academic scholarship. Over the previous twelve years I had been taught by about thirty different teachers. I learned more from some of them than I did from others, I liked some more than others. But what all my teachers shared was a commitment to the government school program, and each of them did well in teaching within the bounds of government-set guidelines.

For my teachers, staying within the guidelines meant, among other things, that no theological (or atheological) stance would be advocated in the classroom. In fact, there were almost no references to God at all. But there were certainly references to other things. I learned trigonometry and differ-

ential Calculus in math classes. I learned about the Renaissance and the War Between the States in history classes, and
of the anatomy of a frog in Biology class. Never in any of
these classes was there a reference to Jesus Christ. Nor did I
expect there to be such a reference, for at the time it would
have seemed out of place to discuss Him. Religion had nothing to do with these subjects, or so I thought.

In not mentioning God, my public school teachers
preached a thundering sermon every day. By implication, they
taught that God is not relevant to most areas of life. The
most destructive things I was taught in the government schools
were *not* the outright lies that were presented (*e.g.*, I descended
from apes, the Puritans were nasty people, *etc.*). These obvious falsehoods can be easily corrected. The most destructive
things I was taught were, by far, the subtle lies about the
character of God. Daily I was taught that two and two are
four, the Declaration of Independence was signed in 1776,
and that frogs breathe in water, *regardless of whether Jesus Christ
is Lord over such matters.* Every lesson attempted to debunk
the clear teaching of Scripture that Jesus Christ is the one "in
whom are hidden all the treasures of wisdom and knowledge"
(Col. 2:3).

I had believed in God since childhood, and I never relin-
quished this belief. But with every lesson, in every class period, all day every day for twelve years, I was being taught to
think like an atheist in the academic realm. And I didn't even
know that I was being indoctrinated.

The results of such constant exposure to unbiblical, "God-
neutral" thinking in my own mind should not have been surprising at all. Jesus taught, "A disciple is not above his teacher,
but everyone who is perfectly trained will be like his teacher"
(Luke 6:40). Having been trained for twelve years in the government schools, where *as a matter of principle* Christ is not
exalted as Lord over all things, I naturally had no idea of the
lordship of Christ. To me, Christ had become relevant only
to very narrow conceptions of morality and worship—

churchy stuff—and yet I still thought that I was a good Christian. I was not; I was a student who had been perfectly trained to become like his teacher.

God graciously called me out of my academic futility. I now teach in a Christian school where Christ is acknowledged as Lord in every area of study. In that capacity I have seen a tremendous need for both teachers and students to beware of slipping into unbiblical patterns of thought—even in Christian schools. Scripture clearly states how this is to be done—by "bringing every thought into captivity to the obedience of Christ" (2 Cor. 10:5). This includes every mathematical thought, every historical thought, every artistic thought, *etc.* This essay introduces this kind of thinking.

This essay is about Differential Calculus, Botany, Renaissance History, Hebrew Grammar, and numerous other areas of academic pursuit. But only indirectly. The focal point here is to provide a very basic foundation for all these areas of study. The foundational questions behind all academic inquiries can be reduced to three very basic ones: What is real? What is true, and how do we know it? and, What is good? All worldviews have answers to these questions, but not all of them provide *adequate* answers.

Consider the following basic beliefs, which most people regard as axiomatic: two contradictory statements cannot both be true; nature behaves uniformly; human beings should be treated with dignity; division by zero is invalid; similar events recur in history; sensory perceptions reflect objective reality. Such claims are so taken for granted that few bother to justify them. Are they true? If so, how would we know? Will just any view of reality, knowledge, or ethics provide adequate justification for these claims that we all take for granted in our everyday experience?

All worldviews purport to make some sense of everyday experience, and the Christian worldview is no exception. In fact, the Scriptures claim that *only* the Christian worldview is sensible, and that all others are foolish (*e.g.*, 1 Cor. 1:20). What is this glorious Christian worldview that is so central to education? How does it differ from its competitors? The following overview addresses these questions. Its organization covers the three most basic building blocks of any worldview, the areas of reality, knowledge, and ethics.

The Christian View of Reality

Two biblical doctrines are essential distinctives of the Christian view of reality. These are the doctrines of Creation and Providence. These doctrines teach that God is absolute, and *only* He is absolute. A unique understanding of man follows from this, as we shall see.

The Bible teaches that God created the universe, and that He did so of His own free volition. The Christian doctrine of Creation does not suggest, as some have held, that God needed to create, that He somehow lacked something that could only be corrected by creating a universe. God is self-sufficient and autonomous. He is in no way dependent upon the created universe. This is true even as we consider God as Creator. For the universe, by contrast, is utterly dependent upon God. It even depends upon Him for its structures and laws. Moreover, the makeup of the universe is patterned after the character of its Creator; God is not the author of rebellion against Himself. The universe is His and His alone, and it everywhere bears His signature as its Creator and Owner. The heavens and the firmament declare God's glory to the earth (Ps. 19:1ff.), and the earth is full of His glory as well (Is. 6:3).

In His creative activity, God has called into existence many different kinds of things. They exist because He brought them into being. He created material things made up of substances that can be perceived by a man's senses. He created spirits: nonmaterial entities that possess personality (*e.g.*, angels, souls, spirits). He also created conceptual, abstract entities such as laws, numbers, and categories. These different kinds of entities function together in the way He decreed that they would, according to His design.

Thus we contrast the Christian view of reality from that of the modern materialist. Materialism does not allow for the existence of nonmaterial entities, while the Christian worldview does. Materialists are embarrassed when we ask them how they can account for nonmaterial entities such as laws of logic, numbers, and categories, all of which they constantly use.

The doctrine of Creation also sets Christianity apart from Pantheism. Pantheists identify God with nature; God's attributes are seen as the properties of nature. They may believe in one Great Spirit or in numerous nature-deities, or even a combination of the two. In either case, nature is deified. Many native American cultures are pantheistic, as are our modern "mother-earth" environmentalists. Pantheism is patently anti-Christian because it maintains no sharp distinction between Creator and creature.

Along with Creation, the Bible teaches the doctrine of Providence. If we accepted the doctrine of Creation alone, and excluded Providence, the universe would have been created and designed by God but then left alone to continue running on its own steam. This is precisely what the Deists taught in the Enlightenment. The Bible claims that the Christian God not only created, but also that He governs everything that comes to pass. His decrees are irrevocable; He alone is in ultimate control. Yet though He is over all things (transcendent), He is not aloof and uninvolved with His creation. His providential oversight is *immanent* and *personal*. At all times, He is intimately acquainted with and relates to everything in His universe.

The doctrines of Creation and Providence address the relationship of the created universe to its Creator. Neither creation as a whole, nor any part of creation, is autonomous (self-governing). Only God is autonomous, and all of creation is dependent upon and subject to Him.

One specific Creator-creature relationship deserves particular attention. Perhaps the most sublime of all of these relationships is the one God has established between Himself and man. Man is unique in that He was created by God as His image-bearer. God commanded man to fill the earth and to subdue it, and to have dominion over it. Thus God established man as His steward over the earth. Naturally, man is given various prescriptions and charges to fulfill as he dwells on earth: laws for proper worship; for just and equitable commerce; for family, civil, and church responsibilities; and for personal piety.

The first man did not follow God's prescriptions (*i.e.*, His Law) even though God had created him and was his rightful owner. All men since have followed in the steps of the first man, rebelliously presuming themselves to be the ultimate expressions of reality. They carried on their rule over the earth in futility, following their own law rather than God's. Such rebellion justly warrants the wrath of God, and so God condemned man. In His mercy, however, God the Father sent His Son, who is fully God and fully man, to live a completely righteous life. He then endured the just sentence of death in the stead of rebellious men. According to this propitiation, and the imputation of the Son's righteousness to these men, those for whom He died are justified; they are restored to legal favor before God.

The doctrines of Creation and Providence are central to the Christian view of reality. These doctrines declare God to be the ultimate reality and the determiner of what is and what is not real. These notions have an important bearing upon the Christian view of man (anthropology). Man is God's creature and is subject to and dependent upon God in all things. Every man is subject to God, regardless of whether he owns up to this fact or rebelliously denies it.

The Christian View of Knowledge

As with the Christian view of reality, the Christian view of knowledge begins with God. God has complete knowledge of Himself. Thus to understand Himself He need not (as many would suggest) know Himself only as He stands in reference to other things. He is *self-referential*. God does not know Himself to be a God of truth because He sees Himself measure up to a more ultimate standard of truth that exists beyond Him. When we speak of God as a God of truth, we mean that God is truth. Truth is defined by His own perfect councils.[†]

Thus God also has exhaustive knowledge of creation. He is omniscient, but not because He inquires and "finds out" about matters in the way a man would. Since God created and governs all creation, He knows all things because He originally conceived all things. Thus we say that God's knowledge, in contrast to man's, is original.

Man attains knowledge in an utterly different manner. Unlike God, man does not conceive things originally. When man discovers truth, whether it be "2+2=4," "Washington was the first president," or "Jesus is Lord," he only discovers what God has known all along. Augustine stated the matter well by saying that man thinks God's thoughts after Him.

Moreover, man cannot *truly know* anything unless he understands it in reference to the God who originally conceived it. To illustrate, note that everyone believes that some connection exists between the universal abstraction, "2+2=4," and the two pairs of apples we see on a table. But only Christianity can account for the connection. By persistently refusing to appeal to the orderly mind of God and His governance over creation, non-Christian philosophers have always been

---

[†] Here we distinguish Christian epistemology from that of other forms of theism. The gods of the Greeks and Romans, and those of the Far East (*e.g.*, Hinduism), are not self-referential. Even the Roman Catholic notion of God (as it was taught by Aquinas) is articulated in relation to a more ultimate notion of "being;" thus the God of Catholicism is not self-referential. A proper understanding of God, and thereby a basis for sound epistemology, is only preserved in theology of classical Protestantism.

embarrassed in their vain attempts to account for a connection that we all take for granted between abstract, universal numbers and material, individual things that we see and feel. While they continue to believe that two apples added to two other apples make four apples, honest philosophers have confessed that they have no idea why.

Since God is Lord over all creation, nothing is truly intelligible to men unless it is understood in reference to God. This concurs with the Christian view of reality, in which God is the ultimate reality from whom every existing thing is derived, and that every existing thing testifies to His character. So we see in the Christian view of knowledge that God is the ultimate truth from which all meaning is derived.

We must still go further. Having shown that God and His counsels are the foundation of all meaning, now we need to discuss how man comes to understand meaning. In doing so, bear in mind the Christian view of man discussed in the previous section. Noted there was the truth that man's existence and continuing life is utterly dependent upon God. Since man depends on God for everything, he certainly depends on Him to acquire knowledge. According to the Christian view, *man comes to know only by revelation from God*. Man can know nothing that God did not reveal to him. Several observations should be made about this revelation.

First, knowledge is revealed to man *through Christ* (*cf.* Col. 2:3). While God is infinite, man is finite. God is unchanging, man changes constantly. How can there be any point of contact between God and man? In His Son, Jesus Christ, God mediates between the two. Hence, all knowledge is *Christian* knowledge. Christ is Immanuel, "God-with-us" (Is. 7:14). In Him the fullness of the Godhead dwells bodily (Col. 2:9). He is the Word of God who dwelt among us and we beheld His glory (Jn. 1:14). Though no one has seen God at any time, the Son has declared Him (Jn. 1:18). In Him and by Him we see the glory of the One who is full of truth (Jn. 1:14). God has spoken to us by his Son, the radiance of His glory and the exact representation of His being (Heb. 1:2-3). Moreover, in Him is hidden all treasures of wisdom and knowledge (Col. 2:3). Christ is the point of contact between God and man, and through this contact God imparts knowledge to man. Ultimately, to reject Christ is to renounce knowledge.

Because of Christ the mediator, even finite, temporal, changing man can come to know absolute, universal, and unchanging truths. These include logical and mathematical laws, absolute ethical norms, objective categories in language, and the inherent properties of matter. Non-Christian thought can account for none of these.

Though they reject Christ, unbelievers depend upon Him for knowledge all the same. All things were created by Christ and for Christ (Jn. 1:3; Col. 1:16). Included in creation is man's capacity to know. Moreover, God causes all men to know some things. In creation God's attributes are revealed (Rom. 1:19-20), and He gives good gifts to men, even to unbelievers (Matt. 5:45; Acts 14:17). But they suppress this knowledge, so their thinking has become futile (Rom. 1:18, 21); their hardened hearts have darkened their understanding, rendering them ignorant (Eph. 4:18). To a Christian, "all triangles are three-sided" and "Napoleon was defeated at Waterloo" testify to the wisdom of God. To the unbeliever who remains true to his rebellion, these ideas, like everything else in his worldview, are nonsense.

In discussing the Christian view of knowledge, we began by recognizing the ultimacy of God. He determines what is true based on His divine counsels, and He sets the standards and parameters for any enquiry into what is true. All that a man can possibly know to be true is nothing more than what God has revealed to him. Just as the Christian view of reality begins with God and centers around Him, so the Christian view of knowledge does the same. From here we may easily move on to Christian ethics where this trend continues. Ethics is the third and final area in our description of the Christian worldview.

The Christian View of Ethics

Ethics is the study of right and wrong and the justification of moral claims. The previous sections relate God's ultimacy in the areas of reality and knowledge. Correspondingly, in ethics we shall deny that there is any ethical standard above God or alongside God. God alone is the standard. He is therefore the ultimate good.

Since the time of Socrates and Plato people have understood that God is good. But why is He good? The Greeks taught that Zeus is good because he meets a standard of goodness that somehow exists above or alongside Him. But the God of Christianity is no Zeus. *The Bible teaches that God's character defines goodness.* According to the Christian view it is absurd to even suggest, as many unbelievers do assert, that God may have done an evil act at some time. Doing evil is impossible for God; God is good, and He cannot deny Himself. Just as it is absurd, by definition, to speak of a round triangle, so it is absurd to speak of an evil act of God.

An implication of this view of God as the ultimate ethical standard is that God's value system cannot be judged by man or by any other standard. Rather, God's character is the basis for all ethical judgments. His Word reveals ethical standards and makes ethical judgments possible for men. A good deed can be rightly spoken of as "good" only if God has declared it to be good. And this declaration is laid down infallibly in His Word.

Unfortunately, many well-meaning Christians abandon this point and adopt humanistic or naturalistic ethical standards when they confront the world. For instance, homosexuals argue that their sexual orientation is determined by "nature," and since their orientation is natural it must be good. Many Christians challenge this argument by appealing to the same standard that the homosexual does: a materialist-scientific view of nature. When they argue that homosexuality is wrong ultimately because it is unnatural, then they tacitly accept the notion that nature, autonomously understood, determines what is and what is not evil. Such "Christian" argumentation denies the ultimacy of God in ethics, and instead affirms the ultimacy of nature. The creature replaces the Creator. A more biblical response to the homosexual argument would be to dismiss as irrelevant whether or not homosexual orientation is naturally determined. In fact, Scripture teaches that all sin is natural to the carnal man. A sound Christian witness to the issue would charge that nature *alone* does not establish standards of right and wrong. Only the Christian God establishes such standards.

Summary

We may now summarize the Christian worldview. The heart of the Christian worldview is the ultimacy of God in reality, knowledge, and ethics. God is the final and eternal Reality who created all else that exists; all reality is derived from Him. In Him all reality coheres. God is also the ultimate, independent standard of truth. From Him all meaning is derived: all relationships, whether cause-effect, chronological or categorical, are established by Him and are made known as He reveals them. Included among these relationships are the ethical distinctions of good and evil, just and unjust, *etc.* Thus as He is ultimate Reality and ultimate Truth, God is also the ultimate ethical Good.

Whatever might rightly be called an education must teach the lordship of Christ. Any subject treated apart from Christ fails to meet the basic goal of education: to impart knowledge. Apart from Christ there is no education, for without Him knowledge is impossible. A Christian curriculum must include study in Christ's lordship, and the study must not be restricted to a theology course. As Lord, His dominion is to be studied in mathematics and logic, the sciences, and the arts. Falling short of such instruction denies His lordship and stands against the fundamental purpose of education.

FIVE:

Worldview Test Case: Christianity in Math Class
Jim Nance

O Thou Who dost by the light of nature promote in us the desire for the light of grace, that by its means Thou mayest transport us into the light of glory, I give thanks to Thee, O Lord Creator, Who hast delighted me with Thy makings and in the work of Thy hands have I exulted. Behold! now, I have completed the work of my profession, having employed as much power of mind as Thou didst give to me; to the men who are going to read those demonstrations I have made manifest the glory of Thy works, as much of its infinity as the narrows of my intellect could apprehend . . . and finally deign graciously to effect that these demonstrations give way to Thy glory and the salvation of souls and nowhere be an obstacle to that.

Johannes Kepler,
Harmonies of the World

Christian schools should have the goal of teaching *all* subjects as part of an integrated whole with the Scriptures at the center. Included in these subjects is mathematics. In no way should Christians believe the lie that, though history, literature, science, and other subjects can be successfully integrated with the Christian worldview, mathematics is somehow worldview neutral. On the contrary, mathematics is a very theological science, being an expression of the numeric aspect of God's character and of the logic that is in Him. In the preface to his *Almagest*, Ptolemy wrote that the mathematical sciences were the best evidence of divinity because of their consistency and incorruptibility. Mathematics seeks to discover, examine and apply those fundamental laws by which God gives order to His creation.

Before we consider in more detail the Christian worldview of mathematics, we will find it useful to examine various philosophical problems resulting from an unbelieving approach to this subject.

No Neutrality

The first problem of unbelieving mathematics is *the myth of neutrality*. Many unbelievers (and unfortunately some Christians as well) insist that, though many areas of study are influenced by presuppositions and worldviews, surely mathematics remains unaffected. Here at least, they say, is a neutral area where people of all different beliefs can agree. "Everyone agrees that $1 + 1 = 2$ regardless of individual religious convictions." "Students can learn about calculus without any reference to deity."

Such attitudes are not borne out by the facts. Not everyone agrees on even the most fundamental of mathematical truths. One plus one equals two only if the numbers one and two reflect something about reality. This has been challenged or denied outright by many philosophers throughout history. Vedantic Hinduism, for example, teaches that "in the context of the ultimate truth there is nothing else but pure Spirit. This is the highest point of realization. And one who comes to attain the highest truth knows of no duality."[1] Because Hindus believe that, at the most basic level of reality, all is *one*, they must deny the reality of all other numbers. If you insist that "$1 + 1 = 2$" to such people, they will declare that

---

[1] Balbir Singh, *The Philosophy of the Upanishads* (New Delhi, India: Arnold-Heinemann Publishers, 1983), p. 92.

you are sadly subject to illusion and have been unduly influenced by western philosophy. We can see that the claim of universal agreement in mathematical concepts is just not true.

As we might expect, the more complex our mathematical ideas, the more disagreement we find among thinking men. Do imaginary numbers exist? If so, why are they called imaginary? If not, why are they so useful? Do differentials exist? If they do, then in some way an infinite number of points fits within a finite length. If they do not, then the foundation for calculus is shaken. Men take different sides on such questions due to their different worldviews. Such mathematical concepts are not worldview neutral.

The claim of neutrality in mathematics is internally inconsistent. To maintain that God has nothing to do with mathematics, that math can be taught truly without reference to Him, is to make a very *non-neutral* mathematical claim. I believe that without an omniscient, sovereign, trinitarian Creator and Sustainer of the universe, mathematical claims are uncertain, unreliable, and ultimately nonsensical. This is obviously not a neutral position. But anyone who would disagree with me can do so only on the basis of their *own* non-neutral beliefs. And to say that math ought not to be influenced by religious belief is itself a religious belief about math, and thus is a blatant self-contradiction.

Neutrality in math also has epistemological problems. Without a God who knows all things, no mathematical truth could be confidently known. How can you be sure of the truth of $1 + 1 = 2$? The question may seem a bit ridiculous, but men have been confident, and wrong, about similarly simple notions in the past. How does the unbeliever know that some greater truth will not be discovered to throw $1 + 1 = 2$ off a bit? But the believer recognizes that God knows all things that can be known, and we trust his revelation to us in such matters. To assert that mathematical truths are unaffected by God's knowledge of them is to claim an awareness of everything which God's knowledge concerns, and that it doesn't concern this. The denial of God's omniscience, with a simultaneous absolute assurance of mathematical truth, is itself a claim to omniscience.

The Mystery of Applicability

The second problem of unbelieving mathematics is even more startling, because many thinking unbelievers have recognized it as an unanswerable problem. This problem is *the mystery of applicability*. This mystery results from asking the question, "Why is mathematics so incredibly effective?" Mathematicians and scientists have stumbled over this question for generations. Why can a few basic equations predict the motions of planets, the paths of projectiles, and so on? If mathematics is man-made, merely a product of human thought, why does it reflect the way the universe works? Morris Kline, author of *Why Johnny Can't Add*, states the problem this way: "To thoughtful scientists it has been a constant source of wonder that nature shows such a large measure of correlation with their mathematical formulas."[2]

An example may clarify the mystery. Imagine you are playing number games. You start with 1 and 1, and add them together to get 2. You add that to the previous number and get 3. Add that to the previous number and you obtain 5. Continue this procedure and the result is the following sequence:[3]

1, 1, 2, 3, 5, 8, 13, 21, 34, 55, 89, 144, 233, 377, 610, 987, 1597 . . .

Now, what is so special about this sequence? Plenty. Examine a pine cone and you will see two spirals winding around it in opposite directions. Count the spirals, and guess what,

---

[2] Morris Kline, *Mathematics and the Search for Knowledge* (New York, NY: Oxford University Press, 1985), p. 227.
[3] Many of you will recognize this as the famous Fibonacci sequence, discovered by Leonardo of Pisa in the thirteenth century.

the number of spirals is always two consecutive numbers in this sequence, such as 5 and 8, or 8 and 13. This is no mere coincidence. The same is true of the center of sunflowers (which have 55 spirals one way and 89 the other), daisies, artichokes, and many other naturally occurring spirals. Examples of this pattern of numbers in nature abound. This sequence and its ramifications find application in such diverse areas as computer programming, architecture, biology, music, and quantum mechanics!

How such mental number games can be so amazingly applicable in the physical world is the mystery of applicability. Norman Campbell, a British physicist, writes about scientific formulas, "But why do they predict? We return once again to the question which we cannot avoid. The final answer that I must give is that I do not know, that nobody knows, and that probably nobody ever will know."[4] Mathematicians like Dr. Campbell, because they do not give the glory to God, cannot explain why math works. Eugene Wigner, who in 1963 won the Nobel prize for his research in quantum mechanics, writes: "The first point is that the enormous usefulness of mathematics in the natural sciences is something bordering on the mysterious and that there is no rational explanation for it."[5]

Given such acknowledgments of this mystery, Morris

---

[4] Norman Campbell, *What is Science?* (New York, NY: Dover Publications, 1953), p. 71.

[5] Eugene Wigner, *Symmetries and Reflections: Scientific Essays* (Bloomington & London: Indiana University Press, 1967), p. 223. He goes on to say on the next page, "The great mathematician fully, almost ruthlessly, exploits the domain of permissible reasoning and skirts the impermissible. That his recklessness does not lead him into a morass of contradictions is a miracle in itself: certainly it is hard to believe that our reasoning power was brought, by Darwin's process of natural selection, to the perfection which it seems to possess. However, this is not our present subject."

Kline admits the following: "Indeed, faced with so many natural mysteries, the scientist is only too glad to bury them under a weight of mathematical symbols, bury them so thoroughly that many generations of workers fail to notice the concealment."[6] What mathematicians do is inexplicable without God in back of it all. Yet rather than admit that they have an unanswerable problem, many scientists hide their bewilderment behind a facade of confident obscurity. The emperor has no clothes, and thinking mathematicians know it. Applied mathematics makes sense only with God-centered presuppositions and if mathematicians continue to build on unbelieving foundations, it will all come tumbling down.

The True Foundation

Not all mathematicians and philosophers of mathematics ignore its true foundation. Many Christian thinkers throughout the ages have recognized and given proper glory to the Lord of mathematics. Nicolaus Copernicus wrote, in his *Revolutions of Heavenly Spheres*, "For who, after applying himself to things which he sees established in the best order and directed by divine ruling . . . would not wonder at the Artificer of all things, in Whom is all happiness and every good."[7]

Isaac Newton is believed by many to be the greatest scientist who ever lived. He laid the groundwork for modern physics, discovered the composition of light, developed calculus, and also wrote commentaries on the Scriptures. Newton wrote in his *Mathematica Principia*: "This most beautiful system of the sun, planets, and comets, could only proceed from the counsel and dominion of an intelligent and powerful Being . . . This Being governs all things, not as the soul of

---

[6] Kline, *Mathematics and the Search for Knowledge*, p. 146.

[7] Nicolaus Copernicus, *Revolutions of Heavenly Spheres*, in *Great Books of the Western World*, Vol. 16, Robert M. Hutchins, ed. (Chicago, IL: Encyclopedia Britannica, 1952), p. 510.

the world, but as Lord over all."[8]

Gottfried Leibniz, a contemporary of Newton and co-developer with him of calculus, said that "it is especially in the sciences and the knowledge of nature and art that we see the wonders of God, his power, wisdom, and goodness . . . That is why, since my youth, I have given myself to the sciences that I loved."[9]

More recently Cornelius Van Til wrote, "Science is possible and actual only because the nonbeliever's principle is not true and the believer's principle is true. Only because God has created the universe and does control it by His providence, is there such a thing as science at all."[10]

Vern Poythress, in his essay titled *A Biblical View of Mathematics*, maintains that "only on the basis of obediently hearing the Word of God can we find a proper foundation for mathematics. It is God who sustains mathematics, not *vice versa*."[11]

Given these testimonies, let us consider in more detail the Christian worldview of mathematics.

A Christian Worldview of Mathematics

The foundation of all truth, including the truths of mathematics, is the God of Scripture. The various spheres of math-

---

[8] Isaac Newton, *Mathematical Principles of Natural Philosophy*, in *Great Books of the Western World*, Vol. 34, pp. 369-370.

[9] Gottfried Leibniz, *Ethics, Law, and Civilization*, in *Leibniz Selections*, Philip Wiener, ed. (New York, NY: Charles Scribner's Sons, 1951), p. 596.

[10] Cornelius Van Til, *A Christian Theory of Knowledge* (Philadelphia, PA: Presbyterian and Reformed Press, 1953), p. 193, as quoted in *Mathematics: Is God Silent?* by James Nickel (Vallecito, CA: Ross House Books, 1990), p. 73.

[11] Vern Poythress, *Foundations of Christian Scholarship: Essays in the Van Til Perspective*, Gary North, ed. (Vallecito, CA: Ross House Books, 1979), p. 176.

ematics are expressions of His logical character and His creative, sustaining power.

First, God Himself has a numerical nature. He is one God in three Persons: Father, Son, and Holy Spirit. The unity of God is declared in Deuteronomy 6:4, "Hear, O Israel: The Lord our God, the Lord is one!" (cf. Is. 44:6; 1 Tim. 2:5; Jas. 2:19). The plurality of God is declared in passages such as 2 Cor 13:14, "The grace of the Lord Jesus Christ, and the love of God, and the communion of the Holy Spirit be with you all. Amen." (cf. Matt. 28:19; 1 Pet. 1:2).

Because God has a plural nature, creation reflects that plurality. The ultimate reality is not one, but one *and* many. Creation is real, and really has distinguishable, countable particulars. As King David said, "O Lord, how manifold are Your works! In wisdom you have made them all" (Ps. 104:24).

God created all things such that creation reflects some of His attributes. Thus we have a trustworthy basis for mathematical concepts. Briefly, the countable attributes of God provide a foundation for arithmetic. God is present in space (cf. Ps. 139:7), thus there is true measure and a foundation for geometry. The infinity and immensity of God (Ps. 90:2; 1 Kings 8:27) also give us a foundation for the concept of infinity used in calculus.

Applied mathematics is the process of discovering and using the laws by which God governs (rules and sustains) His creation. Jesus Christ is Lord of all. In Him all things hold together (Col. 1:17). The mathematical laws which describe how things are held together are consistent laws because Christ Himself is consistent and unchanging (Heb. 13:8). When we discover laws in astronomy, we are discovering the laws which describe how God sustains the heavens (Ps. 33:6-9). When we discover the laws of atomic physics, we discover how God sustains matter, "upholding all things by the word of His power" (Heb. 1:3).

Thus the Christian has the answer to the mystery of applicability. The reason that the mathematical processes of our minds relate to the working of the physical universe is that God has created them both. Concerning this Van Til wrote:

> God has created not only the facts but also the laws of physical existence. And the two are meaningless except as correlatives of one another. Moreover, God has adapted the objects to the subjects of knowledge; that the laws of our minds and the laws of the facts come into fruitful contact with one another is due to God's creative work and to God's providence, by which all things are maintained in their existence and in their operation in relation to one another.[12]

We can trust that the facts that we discover to be true today, if we understand them properly, will be true tomorrow, because God is behind them all revealing truth to men through His creation (Rom. 1:20; Ps. 19:1).

As we study mathematics, we should as Christians expect to see God's handiwork everywhere. We should not be surprised to discover mathematical regularity in physics, astronomy, chemistry, and other sciences. Indeed, we should expect the mathematical formulas we derive to have application in the real world, because God has given mathematics as a tool for extending a godly dominion over creation. Let us consider the dominion aspect of mathematics in some more detail.

A Brief History of Mathematical Dominion

The first man was commanded to "Be fruitful and multiply; fill the earth and subdue it; have dominion over the fish of the sea, over the birds of the air, and over every living thing that moves on the earth" (Gen 1:28). Adam was given every tool necessary to do that: food, warmth, health, animals, the

---

[12] Cornelius Van Til, *An Introduction to Systematic Theology* (Phillipsburg, NJ: Presbyterian and Reformed Publishing Co., 1974), p. 65.

materials of nature, and the intelligence and wisdom to use these tools. Included in these is the ability to observe and apply numeric relationships: time, regularity, distinction, space, quantity, and so on. Yet when he fell, asserting his own autonomy over God's, his ability to extend dominion was marred.

Subsequent history demonstrates that when man seeks to explain the physical universe, he does so autonomously, without reference to God and His commands, and is thus hindered in his efforts to take dominion. Pagan civilizations like Egypt and Babylon developed math to a certain degree such that they were able to make true progress. But after a time they stagnated, going no further in their mathematical development. Why were the wonders of the world, such as the pyramids, not just the first of subsequently greater feats? They reached a peak in mathematics, and then stopped or even declined.

The Greeks also made some incredible advances in mathematics by men such as Pythagoras, Plato, Aristotle, Euclid, and Eratosthenes. Yet after a time, Greek advances in math came to a halt. One reason is that they overemphasized pure, deductive science, which insisted on the autonomy of human reason to discover truth. Plato wrote that math was of a "very great and elevating effect, compelling the soul to reason about abstract number, and rebelling against the introduction of visible or tangible objects into the argument."[13] This rebellion against the tangible, against creation as God made it, contributed to the downfall of Greek mathematics. Experimental work was disparaged, and thus false deductions (such as Socrates' "objects twice as heavy fall twice as fast") went unchallenged for centuries.

In the Middle Ages, and especially in Reformation Europe, men began to again assert that God has given math-

---

[13] Plato, *The Republic*, in *Great Books of the Western World*, Vol. 7, p. 393.

ematics as a tool of dominion. They began to study God's creation experimentally and applying mathematics to it, giving glory to God. Thus they were able to make real progress. The greatest experimental scientists in history came from this era: Newton, Euler, Faraday, *et al.* Due to their foundational work, which we are still building on today, we have an abundance of powerful tools of dominion at our disposal: engines, radios, televisions, airplanes, radars, computers.

However, most modern mathematicians are now turning again toward trusting in the human mind alone as the source of mathematical truth. The goal of math has become for many the development of complex theories and formulas rather than the discovery of God's government of creation. Pure mathematicians often purposely seek to discover mathematical relationships that have no connection to the real world; the toast of the pure mathematician is, "May all this work never be applied!" We have left behind the notion that God has given mathematics for us to use. As a result, many professors and teachers of math, and thus students of math, see the study of higher mathematics as useless and senseless.

If we continue to deny the God who gave mathematical order to creation, we will, despite our technological advances and vast mathematical knowledge, lose all that we have gained. We will lose it all in an inexplicably ordered universe which we by faith will believe to be chaotic. The need of the hour is for mathematicians to repent of their autonomy, recognize Jesus as Lord of mathematics, and turn to the God who gives meaning to their professions and their lives.

Teaching Math

Thankfully, much of what has been given to us by God-fearing mathematicians (and the men who built on their work) has not yet been lost. Consequently, much of how mathematics is taught is consistent with a biblical worldview. Believers and unbelievers alike teach that mathematics is dependable and applicable in the real world; unbelievers just do so inconsistently, without being able to account for it. But they work in God's world, and by His common grace, He allows truth to "fall upon the righteous and the wicked alike." But as we teach math, we should do so with the following things in mind.

First, we should teach mathematics for what it truly is: a recognition of the invisible attributes of God which He reveals in and through creation, for His own glory and for the purpose of fulfilling His mandates of dominion and worldwide evangelization and discipleship. We should *not* consider math as a secular subject or a neutral subject which has nothing to do with God and His world. Neither should we simply baptize math class with prayer and Scripture quotes, telling the students to "learn math to the glory of God" without teaching them how.

Second, in our teaching we should show students how mathematics relates to physical reality because God is the Creator both of the workings of men's minds and the workings of the universe. We should emphasize the powerful coherence between abstract mathematical models and physical reality. More practically, we should choose textbooks which derive their instruction from and apply mathematics to actual examples in the world.[14]

Third, we should point out the beauty and elegance of mathematics, giving glory to God. This can be done explicitly at various times during the students' academic career (the most logical time being the beginning of the school year), but can often be subtle, as long as the students catch the subtlety: "Now, isn't that amazing how such a complicated approach can have such an elegant result; how do you suppose that happened?"

Fourth, though this is beyond the "Christianity in Math

---

[14] With this consideration in mind, we at Logos School have selected *The University of Chicago School Mathematics Project* curriculum by Scott, Foresman for our high-school mathematics program.

Class" of the chapter title, teachers should use the trivium approach to mathematics. Teach the grammar of math first: the facts gained inductively through observations of nature. Then teach the logic of math: the ordered relationships of the facts to each other, the abstract principles and their application. Students should be given the opportunity to discuss and debate mathematical concepts. Teachers should be able to answer the perennial question "What is the good of learning all these equations and methods?" Finish with the rhetoric of math. Let the students themselves relate mathematical principles to other areas and to the" real world." They should be given the opportunity to do some mathematical research on their own. They should read (and even write) essays about mathematics.

We should also use the "problem method." Prepare thought-provoking questions to be answered by the day's lesson. Let the students know that something worthwhile is to be learned if they pay close attention. Give the students problems to solve (from their own experiences, whenever possible) before you tell them the answers. As a rule, tell the student nothing which he can learn on his own. Make the student a discoverer of truth; tell him, "*You* figure it out."

Finally, let your work be motivated by a love for God, for we are commanded to love the Lord our God with all of our heart, soul, *mind* and strength, recognizing Him as Lord of all, bringing every mathematical thought into captivity to the obedience of Christ. And be thankful to God for what He has revealed to us, giving Him all the glory.

Section Two:

The Classical Mind

SIX:

Egalitarianism: The Great Enemy
Douglas Wilson

Egalitarianism is simply "equalism," and in its various guises it represents the most potent ideological threat to the Christian faith in modern times. The threat is most certainly directed at genuinely Christian education.

Now of course the belief that "all men are created equal" represents a profound scriptural truth, but the distortion of this truth represents a cultural calamity of the first order. Christians of course hold to a scriptural sense of justice which has often been confused with egalitarianism. God does not show partiality (1 Pet. 1:17), and prohibits us from doing so (Jas. 2:1,4,9; 3:17). In Christ there is neither Jew nor Greek, slave or free, male or female (Gal. 3:28). But the equality of all men before the Judgment Seat of Christ, and the reflective and derivative equality of all men before *our* law courts, and in our worship, is very different from the "equalism" of modernity. Biblical justice requires the same standard be applied equitably to very different men. Humanistic egalitarianism insists that a multitude of standards be applied to men who are assumed by faith to be the same.

The ramifications for education are immediate and obvious. Speaking of the sin of envy which drives egalitarianism, C.S. Lewis remarked, in the voice of Screwtape:

> It begins to work itself into their educational system . . .
> The basic principle of the new education is to be that dunces

and idlers must not be made to feel inferior to intelligent
and industrious pupils. That would be "undemocratic."
These differences between the pupils—for they are obviously and nakedly individual differences—must be disguised.
This can be done on various levels. At universities, exami-
nations must be framed so that nearly all the students get
good marks . . . The bright pupil thus remains democrati-
cally fettered to his own age group throughout his school
career, and a boy who would be capable of tackling
Aeschylus or Dante sits listening to his coeval's attempts
to spell out A CAT SAT ON A MAT . . . Of course, this
would not follow unless all education became state education. But it will.[1]

The influence of egalitarianism can be felt in our reaction
to some of the words Lewis uses here—dunces, idlers, intelligent, industrious, bright, *etc.* Our aversion to such words in
the educational realm goes far beyond a question of good
manners; in fact, by now such expressions are probably illegal. But until we learn to address the egalitarian root cause of
our educational crisis, we will not find our way out.

The problem is easy to illustrate. If God has made children with varying abilities, and He has, the educator is faced
with a choice. He may apply the same standard to all the
students and get varying results—some students who excel,
others who bring up the rear, with the majority in the middle
of the pack. Or he may insist that the process of education
result in the *same* results, in which case, he must apply varying standards. Egalitarianism demands equality of result, equality of outcome. Because this is not the way God made the
world, the world must be rigged if these egalitarian results are
to be realized. For example, if an egalitarian P.E. teacher insisted that all his students must share the thrill of dunking a
basketball, he really has only one option, that of lowering

---

[1] C.S. Lewis, *The Screwtape Letters* (New York, NY: Macmillan,
1959), pp. 167-168.

the net. In other words, the tendency of egalitarian dogma is always *down*. In a world of inequalities, if the educational standards are constant, then the students will achieve very different results. And if the students must be the same, then the standards will have to be constantly adjusted.

Because of this egalitarianism, government education in our country has become nothing more than a very well-subsidized joke. American schoolchildren consistently bring up the academic rear, although they still feel pretty good about themselves. Those students who do manage somehow to become literate are not trained to think. Their literacy simply enables them to read the propaganda which is so generously handed to them. In the realm of basic civic decency, the students have gone beyond the discipline problems of a generation or two ago (chewing gum, running in the halls) to the level we now observe every day with an astonishing complacency—theft, murder, and rape.

But of course these are all just symptoms. At the heart of this foolishness we find the heart of all foolishness: rebellion against God and His Holy Word. For over one hundred years, Americans have been running a gigantic experiment in the government schools, trying to find out what a society looks like without God. And now we know.

In the early part of the last century, a small band of committed unbelievers (Horace Mann and numerous others) set about the task of destroying Christianity in the United States. The engine they selected for this work suited their purposes perfectly. In appearance benign, in reality malignant, the government schools soon spread everywhere. In the main, evangelical believers quickly bought the lie that the common schools were "their" schools and quietly went along with the seduction.

There were some warnings from some farsighted Christians. A.A. Hodge commented that if the public schools were established, they would prove to be the greatest engine of atheism the world had ever seen. And R.L. Dabney warned

Christians that they must prepare themselves for Bibles, catechisms, and prayers being ultimately driven out of the schools.[2]

But such insightful Christians were blithely disregarded by the church, and the committed unbelievers proceeded with their messianic task. If only they could establish the common schools, if they could only banish the one real "sin" of man (*i.e.* ignorance), then they could usher in a humanistic millennium. With Christianity out of the way, the work could begin on a down-to-earth Paradise—a Paradise of egalitarianism. The government schools were hailed as a savior, and it was assumed that the results of this salvation would be an egalitarian uniformity. But like all idols, this school system had eyes but could not see, and ears, but could not hear. And as recent test scores show, it had a mouth, but could not teach.

The idol has toppled, and shattered, and although it cannot be repaired, many still have not given up hope. Some say that we need to get back to the basics, with strict discipline in academics. Some call for vouchers. In a recent State of the Union message, the president called for uniforms in the government schools—presumably for the students, not the teachers. Others say we need to return to the teaching of morality. But why? Which morality? The people who made the mess say that more money is required. But throughout all calls for reform, the goal of keeping the schools functioning as the great equalizer for all our students is diligently maintained. Given the egalitarian goals, Christians should of course walk away. But they, still thinking of the schools as somehow *theirs*, call for a return of prayer to the schools, and the teaching of creation alongside evolution. But Proverbs tells us that a beautiful woman without discretion is like a gold ring in a pig's snout. Why prayer in an officially agnostic institution? Why the teaching of creation in an officially pluralistic institution?

---

[2] R.L. Dabney, *On Secular Education* (Moscow, ID: Canon Press, 1993), p. 26.

Why do we think it is a victory when the pagans admit our Lord, as an option just for *some*, to their pantheon of gods many and lords many? Why on earth do Christian parents spend their energy trying to teach this addled whore how to put on her makeup better? Perhaps it is because she is getting so ugly that fornication with her is now a trial, and sleeping with her is becoming wearisome. But, of course, a longing for a return to the early stages of the sin is hardly repentance. "Lord," we earnestly pray, "this harlot was once good-looking. If it be Thy will, would you make her so again?"

Hard Work

The egalitarian quickly discovers it to be much easier to retard the progress of the brighter students than it is to bring the slower students up to the higher standard. It is easier to do a little than a lot; it is easier to be lazy than industrious. That is, it is easier in the short run—when the consequences of short-term thinking begin to settle in life becomes bewilderingly hard.

One of the few comforts we find through a thoughtful survey of the modern world is the realization that stupidity doesn't work. Those who rebel against God must also, of necessity, rebel against the world He made. The consequence of this is that all who so rebel, eventually lose.

One of the central follies of modern egalitarian assumptions is that education should be "fun." This dictum, unfortunately, is derived as much from our television sets as it is from departments of education.[3] Consequently, many Christian parents take this assumption with them into their home schooling, or when they enroll their children in a Christian school. As a consequence, we tend to evaluate educational progress by the wrong criteria. Instead of evaluating the work to be done, and then working to bring our children to the

---

[3] Neil Postman, *Amusing Ourselves to Death* (New York, NY: Penguin Group, 1985), pp. 142-154.

point where they can do it, we go the other way. We ask, "How much work can our children do while still enjoying themselves?" "I would hate to teach them to *dislike* learning . . ."

But the Bible teaches that he who is slothful in his work is a brother to him who is a great destroyer (Prov. 18:9). Those who substitute anything for work in education are consequently enemies and destroyers of education. The motives may be "good," but the results are always the same. Now of course this is not a call for grim faces in education. But we must stop trying to get our children to enjoy *themselves*, and begin teaching them to enjoy their *work*. If, for whatever reason, we permit slothfulness in education, we are destroying education. And because we are destroying the education of our children, we are in fact attacking our children.

"For if anyone thinks himself to be something, when he is nothing, he deceives himself. But let each one examine his own work, and then he will have rejoicing in himself alone, and not in another. For each one shall bear his own load" (Gal. 6:3-5). We must teach our children to guard against self-deception as they consider the academic work they do.

In contrast to this, our government's education establishment has set up, as one of their primary objectives, the inculcation of such self-deception. "We want all the kids to feel good about themselves regardless of performance." This is egalitarianism with a vengeance. So they abolish grades, distinctions, and standards, all in the name of maintaining the students' self-esteem. If we cannot equalize performance, we attempt to equalize our perceptions of performance. In other words, contrary to Paul, we want the students to think they are something when they are nothing. The charade may continue (possibly) until graduation, when the hapless graduate discovers that stupidity doesn't work, and that he can't either. He has been thrust out into an unkind world, which will only let him manage the kind of cash register manufactured by Fischer-Price.

But if a thoughtful student is taught to examine his own

work, it is right that he rejoice in it. A job well done is truly satisfying. Christian educators must strive to give their students this kind of satisfaction. And this means work. The fruit of such hard work is a great blessing. Moreover, it is a blessing thoughtful parents will want their children to enjoy. "Do you see a man who excels in his work? He will stand before kings; he will not stand before unknown men" (Prov. 22:29). But in order to enjoy the fruit of outstanding work, we can't start instilling good work habits after college. It must start twenty years earlier, and parents, along with the teachers they hire, ought to impose it.

Still, we should notice an important distinction. Good, honest toil, which is hard because it is hard, differs from aimless toil, which is hard because it is boring. We should seek the former, but the latter is worthless. All hard work is difficult, but not everything that is difficult is hard work. But having established the fact that work is good, and that it is also good to teach our children to love honest work, we still must address some practical questions. How much is too much? What should the "work load" be?

First, we must not assume that the work load is too great just because some of our students are struggling. Egalitarianism is pervasive in our culture, and we must not bend to it in any way. Some students will always cruise through the material without much difficulty, and others will have to sweat bullets to get a B minus. This is the way God made the world, and we should rejoice in it. What is easy for one is hard for another. Educators must not establish a course of study which levels or minimizes those differences. Diligent work *reveals* how God made the world, while laziness unsuccessfully tries to blur it.

Of course, at the opposite extreme, some people pile on the work, in the name of "high standards," and then watch all the students crumple. If this happens, the problem is almost certainly with the teacher, level of materials, or both. The solution here is to back off. If, in a class of twenty-one, seven got A's on the test while three got F's, nothing may be wrong in the way the classroom is run. If all twenty-one fail, however, it is the teacher's failure.

Third, we shouldn't determine the appropriate level of work by listening to students' grumbling. In the first place, grumbling is sin and should not be encouraged in any way, and in the second place, grumbling is a wildly inaccurate indicator. Lazy students can grumble when they never had it so good, and diligent students may suffer silently as they try to make your stupid bricks without any straw. But if the students grumble, a good way to respond is to give an extra assignment. The students obviously need practice in doing work cheerfully.

In short, learning how to teach your students to love hard work involves a great deal of . . . work.

Mental Aptitude

Very few modern Christian educators are fully consistent in their assumptions and practices in education. Given our modern situation, it really has to be this way. Most Christian school parents, teachers, and administrators were educated themselves in the government school system. Through various circumstances, they became disenchanted with that system and found themselves involved with private education. Unfortunately, many of the reasons for the exodus from government education were simply symptoms of the root problem. And if the root problem is not identified, it is easy to bring unbiblical assumptions over into Christian education. Christian schools may not have the same problems with condoms in classrooms, but this does not mean they have gotten away entirely free.

It is a task of some importance, therefore, for Christian educators to weed out any remaining vestiges of educational unbelief. I have found over the years that the most valuable lessons I have received in any area have been the result of *unlearning* something or other. This is especially true of egalitarianism in education.

As discussed above, not all students are equally intelligent. God has created all of us to be different, and some of the differences are seen in the area of mental aptitude. We are not interchangeable *Legos*. But it is an article of faith among secularists (actually it is high dogma) that every child starts at the same place as every other child, that the obvious differences between children are to be accounted for on the basis of environment, and that education is capable of removing these distinctions. Moreover, we have a moral obligation to eradicate such "inequalities."

Some may deny that this assumption is one shared by Christian educators, so posing one such scenario may be helpful. What would happen at the Christian school in your area if they began administering IQ tests to the students, and began placing the students in various academic tracks as a result? Does the word *hubbub* come to mind? And how many Christian parents believe that their child can go as far as any other child they may have read about if they, the parents, work hard enough and find the right school?

The educators cannot put in what God left out. Every normal child can be given a good, rigorous education. But each child will not react the same way to this good education. He cannot. About 50 to 80 percent of a student's intelligence is genetically transmitted, which obviously has a direct effect on the process of education.[4] The unbiblical assumption is the belief that God is *fair*, as a secularist would define the word. But a reasonable look at the inequities of creation deals with that.

Given the varying aptitudes, we must cultivate a biblical view of discipline and work. Christian educators commonly make the mistake of assuming that because Christian students are "new creatures," the need for discipline somehow disappears. It does not. We live in a fallen world, and consequently discipline is a constant necessity in every society. It does not

---

[4] Daniel Seligman, *A Question of Intelligence* (New York, NY: Birch Lane Press, 1992), p. 74.

matter whether or not every member of that society is regenerate, as with a school which seeks to exclude non-Christian students. Nor does it matter how large or small the society is. Lack of discipline is a problem in large Christian schools and in small homeschools, and everywhere in between.

It is commonly assumed that if the teachers are Christian (and self-governed), and if most of the students are Christian (and self-governed), then external discipline becomes unnecessary. For example, teachers don't have to be required to get their lesson plans in, students don't have to be required to pay attention in class, and so on. This is a humanistic pipedream. Worldlings assume that man is basically good, and therefore all that is needed for man to do the good is to be informed of what that good is. The wreckage of the government schools shows us that the "goodness of man" is a poor foundation.

But Christians make a similar mistake if they think a relationship with Christ removes the need for discipline. Self-governance should certainly be expected of all Christians. But in the Bible, this is not something that replaces direction, leadership, admonishment, and discipline from leaders. Rather, self-governance is that which enables a student to respond to such leadership and discipline in a godly way. It is an unbiblical assumption that our "supernatural" goodness replaces the need for authority in the same way non-Christians assume that "natural" goodness replaces the need for authority.

This means that because God has made us with vastly different capacities, we must understand two fundamental truths concerning education. The first is that the innate differences are caused by God in His sovereignty over all things, and our duty is to receive them from Him with meekness. The second is that these differences are revealed in the world and in our schools, as they ought to be, through the hard work of obedience and discipline.

What about Learning Disabilities?

The discussion of learning disabilities in a classical context (and therefore, a non-egalitarian context) requires a host of caveats and qualifiers at the front end. Without them, the classical approach can seem mean-spirited and hard, and perhaps even with such qualifiers, the hard lines which are drawn may be difficult for some to understand. By the time we are done, we may discover that qualifications themselves largely constitute the discussion of learning disabilities in a classical context.

The first is that the phrase "learning disability" is objectionable, not because it is laden with worldview ramifications, but because it is laden with *erroneous* worldview assumptions. We live in a culture which is experiencing an acute breakdown in the realm of education—dysfunctional schools subsidized by codependent taxpayers. Because it is easy to do, the current wisdom has settled on blaming the students, who have not been educated well enough to defend themselves. But the overwhelming number of problems in education should be credited to those responsible, who have all the teaching disabilities common to the pedagogically-impaired. An entire industry has been built up around the phrase *learning disabilities* (and other phrases like it), and it has been spectacularly successful. Not only has the blame been shifted, the schools have gotten a good amount of extra funding to take care of the problems. It is as though government school administrators were shooting students in the halls, and then successfully getting funding to attach another wing of the school devoted to hospital care. We must firmly fix in our minds the fact that when teaching incompetence manifests itself in the disabilities of the student, this does not mean the responsibility for the problem necessarily rests with the student's native abilities, or lack of abilities.

The second problem arises when we see that the problem *does* reside with the student. Those differences of ability which do reside in all students are not a problem which education

can solve. Education reveals such differences, it does not resolve such differences. At this point, we may become squeamish and reveal our implicit acceptance of modern egalitarian dogma. Every teacher since the world began has known,
through long experience, the difference between bright, average, and slow students. But in our egalitarian society, describing any student as slow is a sin, and is probably a crime
in most states by now. Having banished insensitive terms,
we account for the obvious disparity between students by
attaching medical-sounding labels to the problems. After all,
many fine people break their legs, get the flu, find themselves
dyslexic—hey, no problem here. "Wise" and "slow" are words
which commonly bring praise and blame in their train. Words
like "dyslexic" and "attention deficit" invite Get Well Soon
cards.

Thirdly, when egalitarianism is combined with the natural parental desire to be proud of the kids—we always want
the average child to be above average, and usually pretend
that he is—the results are lethal to true classical education.
When one student breezes through the material in twenty
minutes, and gets an A on the test, and another struggles and
scrapes his way up to a C, we think there is something necessarily wrong with the instruction. When every student
struggles under the instruction, the problem is with the instructor. But when some find it easy, some find it hard, and
the majority shrug and say they suppose it's all right, the
problem is not with the instruction. This is rooted in creation, and if we resist it, our real quarrel is with how God
made the world. The best educator in the world cannot put
in what God left out. Every teacher and student can honor
and glorify God when the student is educated up to his capacities, whatever those capacities happen to be. We should
be ashamed if we squander our intellectual resources, but not
if God decided not to bestow the same resources on us as He
did for the family down the street. An industrious child with
three talents far surpasses a ten-talent child who does little.

Christians of another era used to say their children could become what God called them to be. Modern parents, even many who are Christians, say that a child can grow up to be whatever *he* wants. To say that any child can grow up to be president is not a patriotic sentiment; it is humanist idiocy. This piece of egalitarian dogma is a lie we have believed, and a lie we have passed on to our children. The lie makes us unhappy when our educational efforts collide with adamantine reality.

This, of course, brings up the issue of learning disabilities, about which a responsible and biblical book needs to be written. Suffice it to say here that "learning disabilities" can be divided into two categories. The first consists of those deficiencies caused by poor teaching, and which can be corrected by good teachers who maintain high standards. The second category consists of those students who have been known by every teacher in the history of the world—students who are significantly slower in grasping the material than other, brighter students. In contrast to the teachers of another era, we teach such students badly and attach medical-sounding labels to conceal our helplessness.

This line of thought brings us to the necessary conclusion—classical education is anti-egalitarian by its very nature. Classical learning is therefore *not* an educational fad, which all parents must consider for their children. Many parents should not consider it. Classical education has high and challenging standards. To say this is not an attempt to establish a snooty country club education; it merely urges parents to consider their child's calling and abilities—not disabilities—before God.

SEVEN:

The Classical Model: Trivium 101
Tom Spencer

During my first or second year at Logos School, we were still trying to develop our secondary program. As part of this effort, we invited the secondary parents to an information meeting to discuss future plans. During the presentation the speakers had discussed the philosophy and purpose of "classical education." After we took questions from parents. One parent asked, "what does classical education mean?" Several attempts were made to respond to this question. Trying to answer the question made us realize, that the board, administration, and staff of Logos School had not yet agreed upon a common definition of *classical education*. We obviously needed to figure out exactly what we meant. Developing a common understanding of this phrase has been a long process. The first source that we used to develop our philosophy of classical education was Dorothy Sayers's essay, *The Lost Tools of Learning*.

Last summer, I completed work on my master's degree in education administration at the University of Idaho. Over the past several years, the obvious disregard and disdain for history on the part of professional educators has intrigued me. So many individuals involved in public and private education never even stop to ask the question, "How did our forefathers address the educational needs of their children?" Today, some individual will come up with some "innovative" educational idea (usually an old idea dressed up in new clothes). This will probably be a theoretical model. Schools across the country will then implement the idea, never asking questions about the previous success of the new theory, method, or technique. Is this not truly amazing? Think about it. Would you consider undergoing a new medical treatment that had not been carefully researched? Would you be willing to purchase a new product the producers had not tested? Why are we so willing to experiment on our children? After four or five years, educators will realize that the new theory is not working. Meanwhile, they have shortchanged our children. We cannot give children their wasted years of education back.

A recent example of these phenomena was described in a newsletter from the Sing, Spell, Read, and Write corporation.[†] The editors reported that after several years of experimenting with whole language instruction, Delaine Easton, California State Superintendent of Schools admitted, "We have made an honest mistake." She based this conclusion on years of poor test scores. Oh, well, they had only been using these methods for the past ten years!

We act as if the past is irrelevant to the problems facing us today. Our society is changing. Information is exploding. Demographics are shifting. We could not possibly learn anything from those who were in the business of education one hundred years ago, or even fifty years ago.

Is there any other field where people are so quick to jump on the bandwagon before asking questions about demonstrated success? Educators do not apply or even consider the scientific method. This is unfortunate and foolish. Certainly the society that we live in today is different from that of our grandparents, and even our parents. *Yet has the process of learning changed? Have students changed in the way that they learn?*

[†] *The Inside Track*, International Learning Systems, November 1995.

Have the characteristics of children changed so significantly that ways that were successful in the past are irrelevant today? I do not believe so.

We have much to learn and we must start by asking the right questions. A study of history reveals the existence of highly literate societies. How did they educate their children? What topics were considered important? How did they teach their children how to learn? As the Teacher said, "Whatever is has already been, and what will be has been before; and God will call the past to account" (Ecclesiastes 3:15). We should start our educational design by looking at what we have tried before, sorting out the wheat from the chaff. We should look for evidence of successful education, great works in art and literature, enduring music. Then, we should look to see how the process of education was completed. Perhaps we can learn from those who have addressed these questions in previous centuries.

Thankfully, some individuals believe that we can learn from history. In the 1940's, Dorothy Sayers found the educational system in England lacking. In an address delivered at Oxford University, Miss Sayers suggested looking back in time for a solution to the educational problems of her day. This essay is an attempt to summarize the basic tenets of classical methodology (as we have defined it).

⟨ The basic building block for the structure of classical education is the Trivium. The Trivium literally means "the threefold way." It includes three different subjects that were studied in preparation for the Quadrivium. The composition of the Trivium has varied at different times in history. For our purposes, the Trivium consists of the three subjects, grammar, logic, and rhetoric. No matter the particular subjects composing the Trivium, one thing has not changed. *The purpose of the Trivium has always been to prepare students for the Quadrivium.* To implement the classical structure successfully, teachers must understand that the students are being prepared for their future educational pursuits. In other words, the measure of the successful education goes beyond the present. The students are given the tools of learning during the Trivium, they apply these tools as they study subjects later in the Quadrivium.

The first stage is the grammar stage. Grammar of course, refers to the study of language. Our use of the word grammar has applications beyond English classes. Each subject that we study has a grammar associated with it. There is a grammar associated with Bible, science, foreign language, history, and math. The grammar is "the fundamental rules of each subject." The grammar of history consists of important events, persons, dates, and locations. The grammar of math consists of such things as multiplication and division tables. When children study grammar according to the classical structure, they are learning the facts associated with each subject area. It will be helpful if students memorize many of these facts.

Dorothy Sayers does specify one subject for study during the grammar stage, namely Latin. The study of Latin provides many distinct benefits to the students. One benefit is the student's enhanced understanding of the structure of the English language. In addition, the child will find many uses for their knowledge of Latin vocabulary. It will enhance their understanding of science, literature, and the vocabulary of other related languages.

The next stage is the dialectic stage. The key component of this part of the Trivium is the study of formal logic. The student in this stage learns the importance of defining terms accurately. They learn the key components of a well-structured argument. They learn how to organize thoughts, to avoid the use of fallacies, and to detect and name fallacies present in the arguments of others.

The third and final stage of the Trivium is the Rhetoric stage. The students will now learn how to express their own thoughts and ideas clearly, in both written and oral forms. The students will understand how to make persuasive arguments and to construct eloquent appeals. Students will learn how to enhance their own work using the tools of rhetoric. They will also develop some defenses against the attempted manipulations by others who employ Rhetorical devices.

This is the structure and format of the Trivium in brief. Remember, although we teach subjects during these stages, the study of "subjects" in not the final goal. Rather, we give the student the "Tools of Learning." These tools will be put to use later on. If successful, the student will be well equipped at the conclusion of the Trivium for the work that lies ahead, namely the Quadrivium. (The Quadrivium is understood to be the study of individual subjects. Historical examples are arithmetic, music, geometry, and astronomy.)

The true brilliance of Dorothy Sayers's vision found in the way she relates the three parts of the Trivium to three stages of childhood that she classified.

The three stages of childhood are the Poll-Parrot, the Pert, and the Poetic. (After awhile, the names will become an aid rather than a hindrance to remembering the three stages.) Children in the first stage, the Poll-Parrot stage (ages 9-11), have a tremendous ability for *observation* and *memory*. Their minds at this time are like empty hard drives on a computer. They are ready to receive a great deal of information. They enjoy the sounds of strange words. The also enjoy recitations, individually and in groups.

The next stage is called the Pert stage (ages 12-14). Think of the typical American junior-high school student. They like to argue. They enjoy correcting the mistakes of their parents and teachers. They are beginning to develop the ability for abstract thought.

Finally, students enter the Poetic stage (ages 14-16). Students finally show the ability to formulate their own creative written and oral expressions. They are ready to demonstrate their desire for independent thought. (A cartoonist captured this characteristic when he drew a world map according to a teenager. The largest county in the world, by far, was in the center of the map. This country was called *Me*. There were some other small countries far off in the distance.) These are the three stages of childhood, characterized by Miss Sayers according to their academic interests and abilities.

Miss Sayers's model is brilliantly simplistic, matching the three stages of childhood to the three stages of the Trivium. The form and structure of Sayers's classical model looks like this. The stages of childhood are listed on the left, with the corresponding part of the Trivium shown on the right:

Stages of childhood	*The Trivium*
Poll-parrot	Grammar
Pert	Logic
Poetic	Rhetoric

Students in the first stage like to memorize—it comes easily. Therefore, they should receive the tool of learning called "grammar" during this time. Teach them basic facts about English, history, science, and most important, the Bible. As an adult, have you ever sat down to play "Concentration" with children in this stage? If you have, you probably lost. I know of one father who was accused by his son of not trying his best during a Concentration game. The father really was trying to win.

While in second grade, my sons have been taught the names of the major bones in the human body. They learn to identify phalanges, tarsals, and metacarpals. The children love the sounds of these words. Although some parents are skeptical about their children's ability to learn this information, they are very surprised to see how much their children can learn. The students learn by chanting the names of the bones out loud together in class.

The elementary teachers at Logos have really grabbed hold of the classical philosophy in the past few years. Walking down the halls you can hear students in different elementary classrooms reciting English grammar or state facts out loud. The students enjoy this. Elementary teachers must be reminded that their work is establishing a foundation for future study. It definitely requires vision.

Student in the Pert stage like to argue, so, let's teach students how to argue correctly. These students will receive the tool of formal logic. They will learn how to structure their own arguments correctly. They will learn to look for fallacies in the logical structure of the things they read and in the things they hear.

We teach formal logic to eighth-grade students. Each year, the eighth-grade students debate the freshmen on the topic of "How many angels can dance on the head of a pin?" Students debate other topics as well; in fact, we encourage all of our junior-high school teachers to have the students debate issues in a variety of classes.

Students in the Poetic stage receive the tool of Rhetoric. They learn how prepare eloquent and persuasive arguments. They learn the importance of style. They apply the tools of learning previously received to the subjects that interest them the most. This is further preparation for the Quadrivium, the study of specific subject matter. Three stages of the trivium plus three stages of childhood equal a time tested prescription for a successful education.

Juniors and seniors at Logos are required to take Rhetoric. During the past two years, seniors have been required to compose two thesis papers during their senior year. The first paper must be persuasive. The second must argue an original thesis. The students present the papers to two or three faculty members. Students must demonstrate their understanding of the subject by answering questions from the staff.

Where do you find a staff equipped to provide this type of an education? Frankly, it will be difficult. Most of us did not receive this type of education ourselves. You may have to look instead for staff members who share the vision for this educational philosophy and are willing to work hard. Staff training will be very important. I recall the first time that we went through the Dorothy Sayers article together as

staff at Logos. We had a difficult time coming up with specific ideas that could be implemented on a day-to-day basis.
However, as Richard Weaver would have it, "Ideas have consequences." Become familiar about the goals and objectives
of classical education. Over time, the staff members will find
more and more ways to implement the classical vision in their
classrooms.

Our recent staff meetings have included an interesting
exercise. We have taken all of the teacher's lesson plans for
one week into the staff meeting. (For example, all of the elev-
enth grade teachers.) We write the word, "Scriptures" in the
center of the board. The daily objective for each class, history, Latin, math, etc. are then written around the word Scriptures. The teachers are then asked to explain two things. First,
how do we apply a Christian worldview to each objective?
Second, how are the objectives integrated with one another?
The discussions have been encouraging. After a number of
years, the staff members (and the principal) are beginning to
understand the connections. We then discuss how we can
best encourage this understanding in the minds of our students.

Dorothy Sayers's model prescribes the form and structure of an educational philosophy. However, her essay more
generally addresses the matter of content. She does indicate
her preference for teaching a few key subjects, Bible, Latin,
logic and rhetoric. One could argue however, that it is not
necessary to teach classical subjects (Latin, ancient history,
Classical literature) to meet the goals and objectives of a classical education. This is one area that differs slightly in the
vision for classical education described by Douglas Wilson in
his book, *Recovering the Lost Tools of Learning*. Doug writes
that classical also refers to the *content* that is studied.

Is this philosophy of education an effective way to teach
students? By what measure do we evaluate the success of this
program? First, education is a long term investment. Some of
the graduates from our first large senior class in 1992 are just

now completing their college education. (Logos graduates have been accepted at Claremont-McKenna College, Dartmouth University, LeTourneau University, Pensacola Christian College, University of Idaho, and Washington State University.) Most who have entered college have achieved academic success. The students do seem to be well prepared *academically*.

What about standardized test scores? Which test is best suited to measure the success of a classical education? Frankly, there isn't one. However, the test results have been positive. The students have done well and the trend shows higher scores over time. Perhaps this reflects the maturity of our program at Logos School. Seven of ten students graduating in the spring of 1995 took the ACT exam. The national average, in 1995, was 20.8 (on a scale of one to thirty-six). The Logos class of 1995 had a composite score of 27.28. To date, eight of seventeen members of the class of 1996 have completed the ACT exam, their average is 24.6.

These results are encouraging. Over our thirteen years of existence, nothing has changed our belief in the value of this philosophy. Students are not only receiving a quality education, but they seem to appreciate the education that they are receiving as well. Our major concern is avoiding working the students too hard. The higher we set the bar, the harder the students seem to be willing to work. We are eager to watch the lives of our graduates. Miss Sayers closed her essay with these words, "For the sole end of education is simply this: to teach men how to learn for themselves; and whatever instruction fails to do this is effort spent in vain."

EIGHT:

The Trivium Applied in the Elementary
Tom Garfield

You would think I could have picked up on the idea far earlier than I did. I certainly have had enough clues presented to me, especially by my own progeny over the years. It should have been obvious when Carolyn, at only three years old, "read" aloud the entire story of Sleeping Beauty into a tape player. She was able to do this, and even turn the pages at the right points, after hearing her mother and me read it to her for only a week or two. (It seemed a lot longer to us!)

Even with succeeding years and children, I was slow to comprehend the idea. Certainly I should have grasped it when child after child beat the tar out of me at the "Memory Game." Good grief! Why couldn't I remember where the dumb mother elephant was? It was downright tough matching the animal babies to their mothers by just relying on my memory!

Yet, there I'd be with my children accusing me of not trying hard enough and "letting" them win. Well, of course I would swallow my pride, and as a mature adult confess to them the absolute, humbling truth; I told them that . . . yes, I just *wanted* them to win sometimes.

By now you probably know the idea or phenomenon to which I am alluding: the incredible, but innate ability young children have to memorize relatively easily, and recall information. Actually, my poor powers of perception notwithstanding, most people recognize this characteristic of young children. The old favorite Mother Goose and other nursery rhymes, the alphabet and other children's songs, and countless childhood ditties have been passed along from generation to generation, mostly by "oral tradition." And for numerous generations of Europeans and Americans, this ability was *the* means used by teachers to pass on knowledge to young students. In one-room school houses across the nation, for example, teachers would spend virtually the entire day, "hearing the lessons" of their students. The students, for their part, would spend the majority of the day, memorizing and/or reciting the lessons. From long division, to the history of the United States, the students were expected to be able to file it away for recall—when demanded. And it was all done without the presence of a single copier or PC.

Thanks to the philosophical descendants of Horace Mann and John Dewey, however, for about the past eighty years, applying this God-given gift to educate children has been denigrated and rejected. Repelled as anathema, or at least as anachronistic, "rote learning" ("doing something by memory, without thought"—according to Webster), like corporal punishment, has been tossed on the trash heap of "outdated" teaching methods by modern educationists. In our era, the educationists have called for "critical thinking', and "higher order thinking skills", whatever those mean. (You see, when you stake out an area of pseudo-knowledge, and call yourself a professional in it, you can make up terms that no else can figure out, too. Try it—it seems to be a major indoor sport.)

Nevertheless, during World War II, Dorothy Sayers made this observation about the marvelous memorizing ability most children normally have: "The Poll-Parrot stage is the one in which learning by heart is easy and, on the whole, pleasurable; whereas reasoning is difficult and, on the whole, little relished. At this age one readily memorizes the shapes and appearances of things; one likes to recite the number-plates of cars; one rejoices in the chanting of rhymes and the rumble and thunder of unintelligible polysyllables; one enjoys the mere accumulation of things." Otherwise known as the "Grammar Stage" of the tried-and-true medieval Trivium, in a child's life this period seems to last from about age four to about eleven years old.

Look at Miss Sayers's description again. Doesn't that sound familiar? Consider just one aspect of her statement—the enjoyment children have in silly sounds. Perhaps Dr. Seuss understood this peculiar love children have, too . . .

> "In the meanwhile, of course, I was keeping real busy
> Collecting the eggs of the three-eyelashed Tizzy.
> They're quite hard to reach, so I rode on the top
> Of a Ham-ikka-Schnim-ikka-Schnam-ikka Schnopp."
> —*Scrambled Eggs Super*

In any case, he certainly charmed, and continues to charm, millions of children with his wonderful-sounding, multi-syllabic words and strange stories.

Before getting into some specific applications of the grammar stage in a real-life, twentieth century school setting, let's consider our students. Our age group is young children—boys and girls of about four to eleven years old. Not only have we been lied to by the educationists about what works in teaching these little ones, we have been lied to about what they are like. Children are fundamentally different than adults in just about every way: "When I was a child, I used to speak as a child, think as a child, reason(!) as a child; when I became a man, I did away with childish things" (1 Cor 13:11). Interestingly, Paul lived in a culture that, though in rebellion to the true God, still used the principles of the Trivium as a means of educating boys.

Further, C.S. Lewis, for all his higher learning, was a true intellectual; he could speak to and about children, as well as reason with adults. For instance, his Narnia series is without equal in children's literature. He knew full well that not only are children different from adults, boys and girls are designed differently from each other:

"That's right," said Edmund, "Cross it and strike up hill, and we'll be at the Stone Table (Aslan's How, I mean) by eight or nine o'clock. I hope King Caspian will give us a good breakfast!"

"I hope you're right," said Susan. "I can't remember all that at all."

"That's the worst of girls," said Edmund to Peter and the Dwarf. "They never can carry a map in their heads."

"That's because our heads have something inside them," said Lucy. (*Prince Caspian*)

Up-front and openly I admit that I am using sweeping generalities in this area. However, if C.S. Lewis can do it without apology, so can I. The above quote brought to mind a communique from the National Geographic Society regarding their annual Geography Bee. It seems they were wringing their collective hands over the indisputable fact that, year after year, 90+% of the winners in the geography bee are boys! Surprise, surprise, now they are planning on doing a study to determine why this is happening. I guess these young men haven't heard of the now mandatory affirmative action and egalitarianism in every sphere of human endeavor. (Logos has had a girl winner in the past, by the way.)

Historically, and in almost every culture, only boys received a formal education. Then, in the western cultures within the last couple of centuries, all-girl schools began to pop up. Separate schools were the norm for quite some time. Relatively speaking, 'coed' schools are a new invention. Why were schools for so long 'gender specific'? (Sorry, the 90's are affecting me.) The simplest and most obvious answer is that, until recent history, people recognized the fact that girls and boys act, learn, and even think differently. Here are some examples:

Ladies first. Appearances are very important to the girls. How something looks is critical. Every detail should be just right. This naturally combines with a propensity to neatness and orderliness. Girls often have views of people and the world that would be considered Romantic, in the classic sense—that is, honor, virtue, nobility are real and important. Relationships, how individuals are feeling about each other receives a lot of thought and attention. These feelings are often based on their intuitions and assumptions; sometimes they're even right. Girls like to communicate . . . a lot! This is done orally and in writing. Expressing their thoughts and feelings comes as naturally as breathing.

It should be no surprise then to discover that girls consistently do very well in the communication subjects: reading, writing (both composition and handwriting—neat!), spelling, and speech. They also excel in drama (check out the gender proportions in any high school drama club), art, and music.

They tend to get far better grades and have better behavior in school than boys do. Why? Modern schools, probably unintentionally, are generally structured around feminine interests: neatness and organization are stressed, most work in class is written or visual, there are neat rows of desks and chairs, as well as cute, colorful wall decorations.

Now the gentlemen: Appearances have little value to the boys; substantive accomplishments carry the day. One-upmanship is part of every male-dominated conversation. "Oh yeah? Well, I pulled out *four* of my teeth at one time!" Achievements matter. Boys would much rather *win* something, than just get a high mark. Competition is their bread and butter. Having their pride hurt is worse than physical pain. Boys love collections of things; it doesn't matter how valuable the things are, they just want lots of them. Boys are sensory-oriented from infancy to old age, I think. Touch, taste, smell, adjust, grab, tear-apart, fiddle-with, and generally manipulate are their bywords. "How does this thing work?" Analyzing and probing are common practices.

With these characteristics, boys tend to do well in the tangibles: science, geography, P.E., history; and the puzzles: math and logic. However, they lag behind girls in earned grades due partly to their slower physical and social maturation, but also to the fact that most schools use few, if any, tangible teaching and grading methods. Competition is often a naughty word.

Since for cultural and financial reasons we cannot go back to the days of separate schools for boys and girls, we, as parents and teachers, need to recognize and teach to both genders' strength within our grammar instruction. We need to allow and plan for their God-given differences and help them learn to *assist* each other, instead of mock on another. Ultimately this cooperation leads to another God-given human structure, marriage, but we'll leave that for another discussion.

As you probably already know, Logos has been committed to implementing the Trivium since we began. However, just in recent years in the Logos elementary grades, I believe we have gotten a renewed vision of what's academically possible with these little ones. We have chanted Latin endings for years in third through sixth grades with great success. But only recently, with the adoption of some new Poll-parrot style English grammar materials, and several other teacher-created applications of rote-learning, recitations, chants, and songs, we have seen some tremendous increases in the kids' abilities to recall the material presented.

For example, our second graders' grasp on parts of speech, attained through constant, clever recitations, has amazed many of our older students. This is due in large measure to our adoption (thanks to a tip from another ACCS school) of an English grammar program called the Shurley Method, from Shurley Instructional Materials. Even though it is not explicitly Christian or classical, it is indeed implicitly classical by the nature of the program. Our third graders have begun doing "State Facts" several times a day. The teacher announces, "State Facts!" Immediately the students take turns popping up and shouting out special facts about each state studied to date. It takes just a few minutes, but they obviously all know the facts by heart and enjoy the exercise. This program was designed by our new third grade teacher, who obviously hit the ground running with a keen grasp of the grammar methodology.

These improvements and innovations have charged me up like few things have in recent years. We are in the process of making these and other new grammar methods a lasting part of our elementary curriculum. Each year, through the work of our curriculum committee and its subcommittees (all involving the teachers and parents with applicable training), we carefully examine a specific discipline—*e.g.*, science, math, *etc.*—as it is taught in kindergarten through twelfth grade. We try to determine how we can bring the teaching and materials more in line with the school's stated goals, specifically the biblical worldview and the classical methods. This cyclic program of curriculum development has produced wonderful improvements in our science, English, Bible, and history teaching.

Below are some specific suggestions of grammar elements within a given subject area that seem to lend themselves to recitation, or rote memory ("Poll-parrot"). These facts, dates, *etc.* are among those building blocks of knowledge upon which further learning is based. We define "Grammar" as "the fundamental rules/data of each subject." We should note, though much more could be said about this, that these grammar elements, once learned, are often best reinforced through the *integration* of material. That, too, is a strength of the grammar methodology; because God did indeed make a cohesive, interrelated, interdependent universe, all knowledge can find common ground. The student's comprehension of the interconnections is not necessary at this stage; that will come in the Logic or Pert stage. It is enough in the grammar level to have the teacher use, for example, an art project to reinforce historical facts, or a science experiment that applies mathematical principles.

Below are some of the grammar elements of the noted disciplines. The examples given are *examples* and not intended to be an exhaustive list.

Subject Area: Themes/Topics for Recitation, Chanting, Song

Bible: Verses, passages, Books, Ten Commandments, Apostles, Tribes, Creation (actions in days), Lord's prayer

History: U.S. presidents, Preambles to Declaration of Independence/U.S. Constitution, Gettysburg Address, Roman Emperors, Western Civilizations (names in order), rhyming with dates/events ("In 1492..."), rhyming with famous people and their deeds

Geography: Seven continents, four oceans, fifty states, state capitals, famous mountain ranges/rivers

Mathematics: Addition/subtraction facts (to 20), multiplication tables, four properties, basic fractions, counting by 2's, 5's, 10's to ?

Science: Newton's Laws of Motion, Basic scientific method steps, simple chemical formulas (H_2O, CO_2), Classifications (Kingdoms, etc.), bones in human body, planet names/order

English: Parts of sentence/speech (nouns, verbs, etc.), spelling rules/"families", vowels, alphabet, phonics, parts of an essay (intro, body, conclusion), punctuation, capitalization

In addition to recitation and chanting, there are other, probably more "normal" looking methods to use in the poll-parrot stage. But even though they may be used in some of the government schools, these methods are worthwhile because they take advantage of the way God has designed children. Clever, creative teachers—both non-Christian and Christian—have used these methods for years. However, a classical, Christian school must know *why* it teaches the way it teaches. Here are some of those other methods that should be built in:

Guided discovering: draws upon children's natural curiosity about the world and enhances their natural excitement to learn; good for science, math, and integrated areas.

Lots of tactile (sensory-oriented) instruction: can be used for far more than just cute songs—one teacher uses arm and hand movements to help the kids remember rock categories! They are still picking up much about the world through using all their senses.

Drama (a personal favorite): involves many natural interests of children; dressing up, playacting, seeing and hearing stories . . . and I bet you can remember who you were in childhood dramas. Memory!

Collections, displays, models, dioramas: allow for very directed "hands-on" research at even very young ages. Who isn't into miniatures, and clever scenes? Good for history, science, Bible, *etc.* Integrate with art, composition, *etc.*

Story-telling: when done well will create images and detailed memories within the children's minds, even without pictures (our Lord was the Master storyteller).

Field trips, guest speakers (with lots of artifacts): provided good structure is planned, these events again tap into the curiosity of children, and they will remember much.

A final note: children in the upper elementary grades, fourth through sixth, are very likely moving into the Pert stage. Allow for more mature activities in these grades. The students can also be expected to do more on their own, given adequate structures. But remember, even as adults, we enjoy and remember information brought to us in grammatical ways. For instance, which is easier to remember, all four verses of a hymn, or a few scriptures you crammed away?

I am very pleased and excited for our current and future students. I believe as we study them more, and seek to apply *time-proven*, successful methods of teaching, methods that take advantage of this God-given learning tool—the ability to file away cleverly organized facts—we can expect even greater educational success for these young ones. It only makes sense: God has designed the world in such a way that when we use anything the way God designed it to be used His blessing is usually obvious over time.

NINE:

The Seven Laws of Teaching

Tom Spencer

Introduction

Is it possible to reduce the art of successful teaching to seven succinct laws? Yes it is. Read John Milton Gregory's masterful book, *The Seven Laws of Teaching,* and you will see that it may be done.[†] Mr. Gregory's tremendous insight into effective teaching enabled him to break teaching down into its essential components. Futhermore, he was able to explain his understanding in a way that is easily applicable and very useful. An examination of some typical classroom situations makes the value of this book readily apparent.

Meet Sam. Sam is about to begin his first job as a full-time classroom teacher. He will begin his teaching career in a small private Christian school. The school has not been in existence very long and is small; therefore, Sam will teach a number of different classes. He will teach Old Testament Survey and U.S. History to the seventh grade, plus seventh and eighth grade English. Sam graduated with a major in English and a minor in history. Although he does not have a minor in Bible, he has received some good instruction at his church and is very interested in learning more about the Bible. On his application, Sam listed several books he had read in

---

[†]John Milton Gregory, *The Seven Laws of Teaching* (Grand Rapids, MI: Baker, [1884] 1995).

his spare time related to the Old Testament period. In contrast, the only history books he read were books that were required reading for the history courses in which he enrolled. He enjoyed writing short stories, and worked as an editor for a newsletter published by a Christian group on his college campus.

Sam approaches the beginning of the school year with an equal mixture of eager anticipation and trepidation. The principal has asked the teachers to write first quarter academic goals for each course and turn them in the day before school begins. Sam starts with his goals for Bible. Referencing the curriculum guide, Sam reviews the material he hopes to cover during the year. He quickly establishes his first quarter goals for Bible. Developing his quarter goals for English takes a bit longer, but not much. Finally, Sam turns his attention to history. These goals require more work on Sam's part. He carefully reviews the table of contents in the history textbook given to him. He takes a long look at the curriculum guide and wonders which historical topics are most important? Not sure, he plans a course of action that will give equal time to each unit, developing a plan to teach the entire textbook from front to back.

This process repeats itself over the next several weeks as Sam writes his weekly lesson plans. While lesson plans for Bible and English come together rather quickly, it takes longer to prepare his history lessons. He begins to outline each chapter as preparation for teaching history. During class, he writes detailed points on the chalkboard that he expects his students to copy into their notebooks. Besides his classroom presentations, Sam assigns the students pages out of the text to read as homework. They also have questions that they are supposed to answer in writing. As he falls behind in his preparation, silent reading and writing answers to textbook questions take a greater amount of time during class.

Sam notices a real difference in the classes that he is teaching. When students ask questions in Bible and English classes,

Sam is usually able to answer their questions. He enjoys being able to take advantage of the students' interest and teach an idea he had not planned on teaching. However, most of his responses to the questions of his history students are either, "I don't know" or represent his best guess, offered to the students without confidence. He also has a difficult time maintaining good classroom control in history, while students in his other classes are well behaved (for the most part). His history students appear bored and lethargic.

The contrast between these classes are obvious. The first law of teaching addresses the critical difference between the history class and Sam's other courses, *"The teacher must know that which he would teach."* The varied results in Sam's classes reflect his personal knowledge, or lack of it, of the subjects he is teaching. A real clue to what interests potential teachers is found in the books that they choose to read on their own. Remember, Sam had not read any history books on his own initiative. Students are excited when their teachers model interest and enthusiasm for the subjects they are teaching. The real interest of the teacher is infectious; correspondingly, so is the teacher's lack of interest in his subject.

> While knowledge thus thoroughly and familiarly mastered rouses into higher action all the powers of the teacher, it also gives him the command and use of those powers. Instead of a feeling of subservience to his textbook, the teacher who knows his lesson as he ought is at home in his recitation (pp. 31-32).

Teachers quickly realize the difference between mastering their subject and knowing enough to stay one day ahead of their class. When you really understand the subject, teaching is enjoyable. Teachers who have mastered their subject know the personal satisfaction that comes from being able to guide their students' study. The violation of the first law is in a bit of a different category than the violation of other laws. Perhaps the fault lies with the decision to assign a teacher to a class for which they were not prepared. In all candor, this is a situation that is common to young schools. However, in seeking to recover an education that we did not have ourselves, we must simply resolve to work hard. If a teacher has a genuine interest in learning the subject, there is hope. New teachers should not allow their limited knowledge to discourage them, but they should be realistic about the work that lies before them. They must assume the role of the student and commit to learning the material. The second year of teaching should be markedly better than the first.

Let us focus more specifically on the lesson that Sam taught in history. Sam is highly motivated, knows how to work hard and is trying to learn what he does not already know. Yet consider the construction of his lesson. Sam read the text ahead of the students. He outlined the chapter. He reproduced his notes on the board, but did not *require* that the students write down the same, although he encouraged them to do so. Sam is learning more history than he ever has before. The students however, begin to tire of this routine for the lessons do not provide much variety. The students complain about having to take so many notes, so Sam decides to reproduce the outlines he had prepared and distribute them to the class. He gives tests that for the most part, focus on knowledge and comprehension type questions. He requires little in the way of creative analysis. The test results of his students concern him. They do not know as much as Sam thinks they should. They answer questions incorrectly from material presented in class. What is the problem?

The structure of Sam's lessons is deficient; the cause again is partly related to a violation of the first law. Sam does not know the material to be taught. Sam also has an incorrect understanding of the role of the student and the role of the teacher. Consider the fifth law, *"Excite and direct the self-activities of the pupil, and as a rule tell him nothing that he can learn himself"* (p. 84). (As Plutarch said, "The mind is not a vessel to be filled, but a fire to be kindled.") Sam was doing the work of the student. He was learning a great deal. Yet the structure of his lessons allowed his students to remain passive observers, perhaps interested, perhaps not. If Sam would revise his lesson plans and require the students to do the work he was doing, test scores would increase dramatically. For example, rather than giving the students prepared outlines, Sam should teach the students how to write outlines. The teacher might then require that the students outline the chapters themselves. They could discover the most important parts of the chapter. Student interest in this type of lesson might not be all that it should be, but that is a different law.

"*The learner must attend with interest to the material to be learned*" (p.37). This is the second law of teaching. Sam's history students are not interested in the lesson. If they are quiet during class and attentive to the lesson, it reveals more about their understanding of respect and obedience than it does about Sam's interesting teaching style. Sam's limited knowledge makes it difficult for him to capture the interest of his students. Mr. Gregory's book provides suggestions for making lessons interesting. For example, he explains "the problem method." It is an effective teaching tool that teachers can apply to any subject area. At this point, Sam should be receiving some assistance from administrators and/or experienced faculty members. Another educator can probably help Sam identify ways to make the content more appealing to the students. Perhaps the vocabulary Sam is using to teach is part of the problem.

"*The language used in teaching must be common to teacher and learner*" (p. 54). This is the third law of teaching. New teachers often overestimate the oral and reading comprehension of their students, perhaps more frequently in classical schools than in other schools. A lesson Sam really struggled with was teaching his seventh grade class about the Declaration of Independence. In his college history courses, Sam was used to a model of teaching that assumed that students would read and understand all reading assigned as homework. He began the year operating under the same assumption with his students. He was disappointed to discover that many students chose not to complete the reading. Furthermore, those who did read the material found the reading difficult. After grading a quiz based on the reading, the dismal results discouraged him. Sam wanted to find out why the students did so poorly on the quiz. He decided to have the students read the Declaration together during class. Sam called on different students to read aloud. He was surprised at the number of times students hesitated in their reading because of uncertainty about the correct pronunciations of different words. Many students stopped to ask Sam for the definitions of words in the Declaration. Some Sam was not even sure of himself. Seeking to apply what he learned, he began to be attentive to the words he used. He frequently stopped and checked for comprehension during his lectures. Sam learned the importance of using common language.

If this trend continues, the lack of student understanding will become a larger problem. Nevertheless, our history teacher has made a good start by taking the time to try to understand what his students already know. The fourth law of teaching, the law of the lesson states, *"The truth to be taught must be learned through truth already known"* (p.68). Successful teachers, according to this law, will relate new lessons to those lessons previously taught and understood. For example, the Declaration should be related to the reasons for fighting the War for American Independence. Teaching should be done in small steps and increments, class by class, grade by grade.

There is one more law we have not yet considered. *"The pupil must reproduce in his own mind the truth to be learned"* (p. 106). One practical application of this law Sam finds a bit intimidating, "Let the reason why be perpetually asked till the pupil is brought to feel that he is expected to give a reason for his opinions." Sam is uncomfortable with this because *he* is not always sure of the answer to this question. As Sam learns more, he will become more confident posing this question to his students.

Overall, Sam has much to learn. It takes time to become a successful teacher. His knowledge of English and Bible will help him experience the joys of success. In time, he will learn enough to transfer this success to his history courses also. This book can be a immense help to someone who wants to master their craft.

The Seven Laws of Teaching is a primary component of staff orientation at Logos. We have developed a workbook that is integrated with *The Seven Laws*. All new staff members, elementary and secondary, are required to read the book, complete the workbook lessons, and discuss them in staff training meetings. We have designed both job descriptions and staff evaluation instruments around the content of this book. But be careful. New staff members can feel overwhelmed as they consider the work required to master each law. Teachers should look for gradual improvement, not expect immediate mastery of each law. It is helpful and important that all staff members, new and old, keep these laws in mind. At Logos, we may review certain chapters together as a refresher course and seek new ways to apply these laws. This is done according to the seventh and final law of teaching, *"The test and proof of teaching done—the finishing and fastening process— must be a reviewing, rethinking, reknowing, reproducing, and applying of the material that has been taught, the knowledge and ideals and arts that have been communicated"* (p. 19). (This is a good reason to give students some type of comprehensive assessment in each course at the end of the year.) Teachers find it helpful to go back and reconsider ways that they might improve their teaching skills. Administrators will find this book helpful in diagnosing their teaching staffs strengths and weaknesses. This is a valuable book, one that you should provide to every teacher and administrator in your school.

TEN:

The Why and How of Logic
Jim Nance

What First

Before discussing the why and how of teaching logic in the secondary school, we must first discuss the *what*. Read the introduction to ten different logic textbooks, and you will find ten different definitions of logic, all of them presenting a different perspective on this particular discipline.

Logic may be defined first as *the science of the formal principles of reasoning*. A science is a body of knowledge systematized from observation and analysis. Most sciences (namely, the hard sciences) observe the more tangible aspects of creation: chemistry observes the properties of substances and analyzes the changes they undergo as they interact with each other; biology is the study of living organisms; astronomy is the study of the heavens. From their observations, scientists seek to discover the natural laws by which God governs His creation. This is true whether or not they recognize the Governor.

Logic as a *science* observes the human mind as it reasons. In his book *The Laws of Discursive Thought*,[1] James McCosh says, "The discursive operations proceed in a regular manner, that is, according to laws. By carefully observing the acts

---

[1] A great little logic textbook published in 1873 by Robert Carter & Brothers, New York.

of the mind in thinking, we may discover what these laws are, and express them in language or formulae. In doing so, we are constructing a science." For example, we can observe Paul's proof that there is a resurrection of the dead: "If the dead do not rise, then Christ is not risen. And if Christ is not risen, your faith is futile, you are still in your sins! . . . But now Christ is risen from the dead . . ." (1 Cor. 15:16-20). We observe the Apostle applying a certain law: If Christ is not risen, your faith is futile; You will not admit that your faith is futile, so you must admit that Christ is risen. We can express this law as a formula, *If P then Q, not Q, therefore not P.* We call this law *modus tollens*, and recognize it as the same reasoning as: If division by zero is allowed, then you can prove that one equals two; one does not equal two, so division by zero is not allowed.

Logic also observes the mind as it recognizes fallacious reasoning. Consider the argument,[2] "All students have two legs. All gorillas have two legs. Therefore all students are gorillas." Now, you recognize that this is funny because *you know that it doesn't follow.* God has created us with the ability to distinguish between correct and incorrect reasoning. Logic, among other things, studies the laws by which we do this. Specifically, it seeks to discover the laws which may be used to distinguish good reasoning from poor reasoning. Logicians try to answer questions like, "Does the conclusion follow from the premises? Is the argument sound?" They try to discover the rules which can help us answer those questions.

If logic is viewed only as a science, it may be interesting to people with an analytical twist to their psyche, but it is not very practical. We must teach logic not only as a science but also as an *art*. We must teach the *skills* of logic.

---

[2] In logic, the term *argument* does not refer to a heated disagreement but to a set of statements, one of which (the conclusion) appears to be implied by the others (the premises).

Mortimer Adler, in his essay *What is Basic About English?* defines logic as *the art of ordering what is to be expressed in language or of judging what has been expressed.* When you try to communicate anything in the form of an argument, logic as an art will describe the order you must follow to guarantee that your argument is valid. Logic as a science discovers rules. Logic as an art teaches us to apply those rules in different situations. The art of logic provides us with practical skills to use as we reason, discuss, debate, or communicate in all ways. It also provides us with rules by which we may judge the arguments of others, to determine whether their reasoning is good or poor.

God has made us such that we reason by means of language. Logic represents the reasoning inherent in language, breaking the language of arguments down into symbolic form (much like story problems in mathematics[3]) simplifying it such that the reasoning inherent in language becomes visible. Thus the structure of arguments is clarified by removing every possible extraneous part, like a biology student dissecting a frog to see the structure inside. By studying the structure of arguments in this way, a separate, symbolic language is created, a language which has its own particular syntax and rules. As a symbolic language, logic is useful only insofar as these rules accurately reflect the reasoning of the language it represents. Logic must deal with the vagueness and ambiguity of languages such as English. Different forms of logic deal with them in different ways.

Branches on the Tree of Logic

Given these definitions of logic, we should briefly consider the divisions within it. First, I would divide logic into two main branches: informal and formal.

---

[3] Though I mention mathematics here, I will avoid the perennial debate as to whether logic is a species of mathematics, or vice versa. But you should know that such a debate exists.

Informal logic may include a wide range of subjects, such as common sense reasoning, defining terms, informal fallacies, analogies, and puzzle solving. A course in formal logic should have some informal logic scattered throughout to add interest and applicability. Formal logic, on the other hand, analyzes argument structure in a more rigorous, limited way.

Formal logic is divided into inductive and deductive branches. Inductive logic deals with arguments of likelihood and probability. It makes conclusions from specific facts or experience. The conclusions of inductive arguments *go beyond the premises*, but these conclusions can (at least in principle) be tested by further observation. Inductive reasoning is the logic of the experimental sciences: "On ten different occasions I have heated water at different altitudes and found that, the higher the altitude, the lower the boiling point. Thus, all other things being equal, water will always boil at lower temperatures in higher altitudes." Inductive arguments are either *strong* or *weak*, depending on how well the evidence supports the conclusions.

Deductive arguments, however, are either *valid* or *invalid*. If valid, the conclusions necessarily follow from the premises. In valid, deductive arguments, if the premises are true, the conclusions must be true. Deductive logic itself breaks down into several branches, such as categorical and propositional.

Categorical logic (also called syllogistic logic) deals with syllogisms, which are arguments having two premises and one conclusion. The classic example is, "All men are mortal. Socrates is a man. Therefore Socrates is mortal." Such arguments are analyzed and proven valid or invalid by various rules, Venn diagrams, and counter-examples. In categorical logic, individual words are represented by symbols, usually capital letters. The argument "No Hindus are Christians, but some men are Hindus; Therefore some men are not Christians" would be symbolized "No H are C, Some M are H, Therefore some M are not C." Many arguments can be put into categorical form and analyzed for their validity.

In propositional logic (also called symbolic logic), entire sentences or propositions are represented by symbols, along with logical operators such as AND, OR, NOT, and IF/ THEN. Paul's argument from First Corinthians 15 was a propositional argument. Such arguments are analyzed for their validity using truth tables, among other means. Much of digital electronics includes the study of propositional logic.

The Value of Logic

As we consider the value of studying (and teaching) logic, I must make one observation. Logic, as we shall see, is as much a part of our thinking as grammar. Yet I have noticed, usually in the introduction to logic textbooks, an almost universally recognized need to defend the teaching of logic in schools. Rarely do I hear a similar defense of teaching English grammar, or read such in introductions to English grammar textbooks. Given the parallels between logic and grammar, I do not understand why this is. Everyone who thinks and speaks uses both. The study of both is an aid to improved speaking and thinking.

Some may assert that if we use logic naturally, without being taught it formally, we have no need to study it. But is this not true of grammar? All children use grammar before they are taught it in English classes. Why study grammar? The answer, of course, is that we study grammar to recognize proper grammar and to correct improper grammar. Even so, we should study logic to the praise of proper logic and the rectification of improper logic.

Perhaps one reason formal logic has fallen into some disrepute is that historically some philosophers and logic teachers have become enamored with "pure" logic, emphasizing logic as a science and neglecting it as an art. As a result, administrators, teachers, parents and students no longer saw it as practical or useful.

Others may put logic into the same basket with sophistry, believing it to be used as a tool to "prove" error. I agree that this has indeed been attempted. But in such cases logic is being abused, not used, and the abuse of logic is no more a reason to reject its proper study than the abuse of drugs is a reason to neglect the study of medicine. Deductive logic, used correctly, does not say anything beyond the premises. Rather, it simply unfolds in a more explicit way what the premises already contain.

Still, "Why study logic?" is an important question to ask. It will certainly be asked by our students and their parents. Implementing logic into a curriculum is not a trivial task. It requires the hiring (or training) of a logic teacher. It takes the place of some other class the teaching of which could be defended. But even more importantly, this question must be asked and answered because as teachers or administrators we will be held accountable to God for what we teach in our schools.

In her essay *The Lost Tools of Learning*,[4] Dorothy Sayers begins to answer the question in this way: "Neglect of formal logic in the curriculum is the root cause of nearly all those disquieting symptoms we have noted in the modern intellectual constitution." The symptoms she lists include the inability of students to do the following: 1) resist propaganda, 2) argue well, 3) follow a sustained argument given by someone else, 4) distinguish between scholarly and slipshod writing, and 5) learn on their own. Sayers argues that the reintroduction of formal logic into the secondary curriculum will help solve problems such as these.

With that, let us look more closely at the reasons for studying formal logic in the secondary classroom.

---

[4] This essay can be found in Douglas Wilson's *Recovering the Lost Tools of Learning* (Wheaton, IL: Crossway Books, 1991), pp. 145-164.

Logic is Foundational to All Learning

No learning, and in fact no reasoning of any kind, takes place independently of logic. *Logic is an inescapable concept.* Suppose you are talking to someone who denies that he needs to use logic. "Logic is a human invention and would be best left forgotten in the archives of philosophy," he asserts. If asked to defend this assertion without using logic, that is, without giving any reasons, he of course could not. The denial of logic is self-defeating. We cannot decide "not to use logic." We can only decide whether we will use it well or use it poorly. God has made us in His image, as creatures who reason. If someone self-consciously refused to use logic, he would limit himself to either silence or nonsense. And even silence and nonsense are attempts to be consistent—which acknowledges the authority of logic.

Logic is foundational to all learning; it is the art by which all communication is ordered. Specifically, logic is one part of the trivium, along with grammar and rhetoric. These three arts are present in all communication, each depending upon and interconnected with the other two. Grammar without logic is meaningless words; logic without grammar is empty order. And both need rhetoric in order to be expressed.

Logic is inescapable. You can't hide from it and you can't kill it. You'd best make friends and get to know it well.

Logic is an Aid to Improved Reasoning

We must first note that the study of logic does not impart the ability to think any more than the study of grammar imparts the power of speech. You do not have to be trained in formal logic to be able to reason correctly any more than you need to constantly take medicine to be healthy—unless of course you are ill. And I believe that much modern thought is indeed ill and in need of a dose of formal logic. Given two men of otherwise equal capacity to reason, the one who has studied logic is more likely to reason correctly and skillfully, catching his own mistakes and the mistakes of others. This is true for many reasons.

One reason is simply that logic is intellectually rigorous. It expands the mind in the areas of argument, proof, and comparison. Logic makes students think in ways they have not thought before.

When taught as an art, logic provides students with specific skills in arguing properly and analyzing arguments critically. Students learn the importance of defining terms in debate and specific techniques for doing so. They improve their ability to express ideas more clearly and concisely. They practice forming valid arguments and discovering and refuting invalid ones. They learn to distinguish between premises and conclusions, both expressed and assumed. They learn to think before they speak.

I should point out that in teaching students logic, we are handing them loaded guns and training them in their use. This is good, except that initially all the guns are pointed in our direction. The teacher finds himself standing before a class of students who not only *like* to argue, but who now know how to argue *well*. Thus it quickly becomes apparent that all the teachers should also be trained in logic, and all the students should be trained to argue graciously. They should be taught to argue in a Christ-like way.

The study of logic also helps the students to distinguish between valid and invalid reasoning. Dorothy Sayers says, "Indeed, the practical utility of formal logic today lies not so much in the establishment of positive conclusions as in the prompt detection and exposure of invalid inference."[5] This ability to detect and expose invalidity becomes very evident once the students learn the names of the informal fallacies. Students delight in discovering equivocation in the letter to the editor, circular reasoning in the science magazine, and the false cause fallacy in history textbooks. The power to recognize and name popular fallacies protects the students

---

[5] Wilson, *Recovering the Lost Tools of Learning*, p. 158.

from illegitimate authoritative and emotional appeals so prevalent in mass media today. They can be confidently objective as they are taught to look at the facts, not at the speaker. They learn to think, "What he says sounds good, but is it valid? And if valid, are the premises true?"

Logic also prepares students to learn on their own. They improve their ability to read what others have written and listen to what others have said, and understand what they mean. They are taught to look for an author's main points and come to terms with him in order to understand and evaluate his arguments.

Logic is an Aid to Understanding God and His Revelation

In his essay *On Christian Doctrine*, Augustine said, "The validity of logical sequences is not a thing devised by men, but is observed and noted by them that they may be able to learn and teach it; for it exists eternally in the reason of things, and has its origins with God."[6] Logic originates with God. It is an expression of His unchanging, orderly, truthful character. God Himself is logical in His thoughts, and our logic is valid insofar as it is a reflection of His.

Paul writes that "God is not a God of disorder but of peace" (1 Cor. 14:33). God is orderly; He has reasons for what He does. Order implies rationality; where there is no rationality, there is only randomness and chaos.

God's *word is truth* (John 17:17), as opposed to falsehood. His word is noncontradictory. And God Himself is noncontradictory: He cannot lie (Heb. 6:18), and He does not deny Himself (2 Tim. 2:13). He does not act contrary to His promises. God is holy; there is nothing in Him which contradicts His perfections.

John Frame, in his book *The Doctrine of the Knowledge of God*, identifies these things for us, and then adds, "Does God, then, observe the law of noncontradiction? Not in the sense

---

[6] Augustine, *On Christian Doctrine*, Book II, chapter 32.

that the law is somehow higher than God Himself. Rather, God *is* Himself noncontradictory and is therefore Himself the criterion of logical consistency and implication. Logic is an attribute of God, as are justice, mercy, wisdom, and knowledge. As such, God is a model for us. We, as His image, are to imitate His truth, His promise keeping. Thus we, too, are to be noncontradictory."[7] Thus God is logic[8], just as God is love and God is light.

Logic is given by God for the purpose of ordering His revelation to us. The ability to reason is necessarily presupposed in every revelation. God has given us minds that use logic for the same reason He has given us eyes that see, in order that we might grasp His word. Charles Hodge writes in his *Systematic Theology*, "Revelation is the communication of truth to the mind. But the communication of truth supposes the capacity to receive it. Revelations cannot be made to brutes or to idiots. Truths, to be received as objects of faith, must be intellectually apprehended."[9] Without logic we could not obey God's commands, since they are given in the form of universal propositions: "All men must repent. I am a man, therefore I must repent." A denial of logic is therefore disobedience and sin.

This is why the writers of the Westminster Confession wrote, "The whole counsel of God concerning all things necessary for His own glory, man's salvation, faith and life, is either expressly set down in scripture or *by good and necessary*

---

[7] John Frame, *The Doctrine of the Knowledge of God* (Phillipsburg, PA: Presbyterian and Reformed Publishing Co., 1987), p. 253.

[8] Compare John 1:1, "In the beginning was the *logos*, and the *logos* was with God, and the *logos* was God." Gordon Clark, in his *Logic* textbook (The Trinity Foundation, 1988), translates *logos* directly across as LOGIC. I do not feel as comfortable with Clark's translation as I do with his understanding of logic.

[9] Charles Hodge, *Systematic Theology* (reprint, Grand Rapids, MI: Eerdmans, 3 vol., 1986), Vol. 1, p. 49.

consequence may be deduced from scripture" (emphasis mine). In order to comprehend any doctrine, we must use logic, since God has communicated doctrine to man by means of language. But also, we must note that the Bible was not written like a confession of faith, and some nuggets of truth take some digging to get at. The truth that there is one God eternally existent in three Persons, though clearly contained in Scripture, is not contained in one place alone. The Trinity is a truth which requires a godly, submissive use of logic to see.

Logic Provides the Foundation for Other Disciplines

Many areas of study relate directly to logic, and thus the study of logic is the proper foundation for studying them.

First, logic is foundational to rhetoric, especially as logic is taught as an art. Many aspects of logic are carried over into rhetoric: the practice of analyzing arguments quickly and refuting them effectively; the ability to organize arguments in a mental outline; the use of different argument types such as *reductio ad absurdum* and *a fortiori*.

Logic is obviously at the core of philosophy, along with aesthetics, ethics, metaphysics, and epistemology. It is foundational to these disciplines, because it is used in studying them.

Other disciplines in which a grasp of deductive logic is essential include theology, mathematics, law, computer science, electronics, and education. Students of formal logic would have a good start in the study of these disciplines.

Logic Hits the Students Where They Are

In our school we teach logic as a full year, five days per week course in the eighth grade. This finds the students in the middle of what Dorothy Sayers calls the Pert stage, which is recognizable, she says,

> so soon as the pupil shows himself disposed to Pertness and interminable argument (or, as a schoolmaster corre-

spondent of mine more elegantly puts it: "When the capacity for abstract thought begins to manifest itself). . . . It is characterized by contradicting, answering back, liking to "catch people out" (especially one's elders) and the propounding of conundrums (especially the kind with a nasty verbal catch in them). Its nuisance value is extremely high."[10]

Junior high students like to argue. Too often as teachers we want to stifle this impulse. "Don't argue with me!" Instead, we ought to take their natural argumentativeness and mold it to godly use. If done correctly, this does not teach them that to disagree is automatically good, as Douglas Wilson wrote in *Recovering the Lost Tools of Learning*, "If you encourage disagreement for disagreement's sake, then you will get disagreeable children. But if you teach that it is good to question (provided the questioning is intellectually rigorous and honest), then you are *educating*." We will teach with the grain if we take advantage of this trait.

Junior high students also like to catch mistakes, as any teacher of this age group will testify. We should teach them to identify different kinds of mistakes: mistakes in facts or deduction, ethics or understanding.

Finally, junior high students like to solve puzzles, not only puzzles in games, but puzzles in daily life. They ask the same questions as philosophers: What is truth? Where do we get our standards of right and wrong? What is the value of learning? They like to question and search for answers; we should give them the proper techniques for doing so. We should give them time for questions and in-class debates, teaching them the methods and ethics of good argumentation.

We should teach students logic when they are ready for logic, and they will not only learn it, they will love it.

How Logic Should be Taught

Should logic be taught as a subject separate from other sub-

---

[10] Wilson, *Recovering the Lost Tools of Learning*, p. 157, 154.

jects (which is how it is usually taught, when it is taught at all), or should it be included as an integral part of all subjects, as some people advocate? For our school, and I believe for most other schools, the answer is *both*.

First, logic should be taught as a separate subject. This is the most practical method for teaching the details of logic. For example, at our school we want the students to learn the names of more than twenty of the informal fallacies. We want to teach them a number of special terms, such as syllogism, validity, genus, species, self-contradiction, and tautology. We want to give them many specialized techniques for determining validity, such as counter-examples, Venn diagrams, truth tables, formal proofs, and truth trees. We want the students to *use* these names, terms, and techniques in all of their classes, but it would be impractical and inefficient to have the students *learn* them in all of their classes. If the details of logic were taught in every class, some would be skipped over, most would be taught redundantly, and quite likely different teachers would want to teach the different names, terms and techniques differently, to the confusion of the students. We also do not want to require that every teacher be necessarily trained in formal logic, any more than every teacher is trained in mathematics or history. If you have separate classes at all, you must have a separate logic class.

Having said this, let me now hasten to promote the teaching of logic as an integral part of all subjects in the junior high and early high school years. The teacher of each course should emphasize the ordered relationships of particulars in their subject. The logic of each subject will naturally take a slightly different form according to the material covered, though the teacher of that subject should attempt to use the terms and techniques in the same way the students learned them in the logic class. Briefly, it could look something like the following:

In English, when students read books of information, paragraphs should be examined for syllogisms or arguments and sentences in those paragraphs as premises or conclusions. Students should be taught to come to terms with the author and to follow his line of reasoning.[11] Students should learn how to write their own persuasive essays using proper argumentation. They should reduce the essays of others by fifty percent or more to teach them to recognize the author's primary line of reasoning. In speaking, there should be many debates in any and all subjects, becoming more formal up through the rhetoric years.

History will provide ample material for discussion and debate. The linearity of history should be emphasized, along with the reasons for this or that decision and the causes of various historical events.

In math, this is naturally the time to teach the more abstract techniques of algebra and geometry. Geometric proofs should be seen as logical proofs, starting with universal postulates and making specific conclusions. The teacher should emphasize the elegance of the logic of math, especially in problems which start horribly complicated and end up simple and sublime.

In Bible the students should have all the basic facts of biblical history and doctrine at their fingertips from the previous grammar years, and should now be taught the techniques of proper biblical interpretation and the development of more detailed Christian doctrine. The teacher should point out that only in the word of God do the students have an infallible source of truth, and so the distinction between truth and validity becomes especially important. They can obtain in the Bible infallibly true premises, and use proper reasoning to deduce biblical truth by good and necessary consequence.

Formal logic should be viewed as the deductive logic course, and the remainder of the science courses as the induc-

---

[11] Techniques for reading in this way are described very effectively in Mortimer Adler's *How To Read a Book* (New York, NY: Simon & Schuster, 1972), chapters 8 and 9.

tive logic curriculum. Students should be self-consciously making inductive conclusions from observations and experiments, recognizing the validity of inductive reasoning from a Christian worldview.

The Teacher of Logic

Beyond the qualifications for all teachers, such as a love of their subject and a love for children, the logic teacher should meet some special qualifications.

He need not have a degree in philosophy, though that would of course be helpful. But before he attempts to teach such a course, he must have a good education in formal logic. He should not try to teach the material by staying two weeks ahead in the textbook. He will not know the material deeply enough and the students will pick up on this very quickly. He will need to have thought through many basic questions: What makes an argument valid? Can a valid argument be made up of false statements and an invalid argument be made up of true statements? Does *All unicorns have horns* imply that *Some unicorns have horns*? Why is *All S is P* not equivalent to *All P is S*?

The logic teacher needs to have God-given skills in abstract reasoning and organization. He should have a knack for solving puzzles. Logic is a symbolic course. Training in higher math is useful here, along with some artistic talent for drawing diagrams.

The teacher must be able to discuss and debate, especially with younger students. He must be levelheaded yet outspoken, able to argue without becoming heated. He must be able to face a roomful of young people with strong opinions and take advantage of that in class discussion. He must be able to see logic everywhere so that he can teach his students to see it everywhere too.

Available Materials for Teaching Logic

Books are first, of course. There are a number of excellent

logic textbooks in print; a bibliography of them is included at the end of this section. Different texts are more appropriate for different age levels. Some are profitable for student use and others only for the logic teacher's self-study.

To see examples of great reasoning students should be given the opportunity to read great books. The best books in each subject should be read. If studying physics they should read in Newton and Einstein, if theology they should get a taste of Martin Luther and John Owen.

For examples of bad reasoning there are all the other books, especially modern ones, along with any other form of modern communication, written or otherwise. The opinion page of your local newspaper is probably an inferno of formal and informal fallacies. The same goes for verbal information. Listen especially for fallacies made by students themselves (which is only fair, since they will listen for fallacies made by you).

There are also a number of games the students can play to exercise their minds toward logical thinking. For the class as a whole, games such as Mastermind (also called Pico Centro), in which the students try to figure out the order of a three- or four-digit number by means of certain clues, are good practice for precise, orderly thinking. On the less mathematical side are situation games (like twenty questions, but don't limit the number), in which the students are given a general statement from which they must determine the details by asking *yes* or *no* questions. Many other similar games are available.

For the individual students, consider allowing them to play chess, solve matrix logic puzzles, or perhaps even play games like Clue. All these are good practice at making conclusion based on premises, and will form logical tracks in the students' minds.

The best activity, though, is keeping up a constant dialogue with the class, questioning them, challenging their assumptions, regularly pointing out their own reasoning, both good and bad. This is what will make logic *real* to them.

ELEVEN:

The Why and How of Latin
Douglas Wilson

Answering the Curious

"Why Latin?" The answers are varied, and it is perhaps a testimony to how far we have to go in recovering a classical mind that the "pragmatic" answers must come first. This is not to say that pragmatic considerations are wrong, but *pragmatism* most certainly is. When students are educated with beauty and truth in mind, they commonly outperform those who are concerned merely with "results." In other words, pragmatism doesn't work and a cheery rejection of pragmatism does. Consequently, the following pragmatic defence of the study of Latin should in reality be seen as a *defiance* of pragmatism.

Latin students do better than students who opted for more sensible courses. The reasons for this should not be surprising. About eighty percent of English vocabulary comes from Latin and Greek, with over fifty percent of our vocabulary coming from the Latin. Two examples should suffice in making the point. The Latin word *sisto* means *I stand*, or *I stop*. From it we derive *consist* (stand together), *desist* (to stop), *insist* (to stand upon), *exist* (to stand out), and *persist* (to stand through). The Latin word *panis* means *bread*. From it we get *companion* (one who shares your bread), *accompany* (same thought), and *pantry* (a place to keep bread). Even though English is not a Romance language, the effect of Latin on our daily discourse has been immense. Given this, we should not be surprised at all when *English* vocabulary tests reveal that students of Latin score higher than students of other foreign languages. When we consider that successful people often share only one thing, and that one thing is a large vocabulary, the reason for our desire for a rigorous Latin program should be obvious.

But a language is more than a pile of vocabulary words. The words must be assembled in order to make any sense, and the way we assemble words involves grammar and syntax. The study of Latin grammar greatly refines the student's knowledge of grammar in general, which then carries over into English. For one simple example, when *God* is the subject of a Latin sentence, the word appears as *Deus*. When He is the direct object, the word appears as *Deum*. This difference between the nominative and accusative case can help a student who wants to understand why in English he should use *he* in some instances, and *him* in others.

The point was made above that over fifty percent of English vocabulary comes from Latin, even though English is not a Romance language. When a student comes to study a modern Romance language, he has an even greater advantage. As the name indicates, Romance languages are *Roman* in their ancestry. These direct descendants of Latin include Spanish, French, Romanian, Italian, and Portuguese, with over *eighty* percent of their vocabularies coming from the Latin. If someone knows from a very young age that he would like to learn Spanish, then of course the study of Spanish is appropriate. But if someone knows he would like to learn *a* modern language, but is uncertain which he will choose, Latin is the best choice. Latin provides a remarkable platform from which to study many modern languages. This is the case even when the languages are not directly related to Latin. Latin is also helpful for studying other inflected languages like Greek, Russian, and German. Having taken both Greek and Latin, in that order, I can only say that I wish the order had been reversed. Latin is a great stepping stone to the study of any language in which the nouns decline.

Latin also trains the student in the essentials of the scientific method—observation, comparison, and generalization. In Latin, little differences between words are not *little* at all. The observation of a word must be precise, and include all the details. It is not enough to know what a word "means." The student of Latin must cultivate an eye for detail because the details of the word mean far more than they do in English. This habit of mind is helpful in scientific analysis. Earlier this century, the great chemist Bauer commented on the benefit of Latin study for the advanced study of chemistry. A professor Ramsey had questioned him on the difference between the *Real-Schulen* and the *Gymnasien*, presuming that his best students came from the *Real-Schulen*. "'Not at all,' he replied; 'all my best students come from the *Gymnasien*. The students from the *Real-Schulen* do best at first; but after three months work here, they are, as a rule, left behind by those coming from the *Gymnasien*.'" Professor Ramsey wondered at this because the *Real-Schulen* students had been especially instructed in chemistry. "'Yes,' he replied; 'but the students from the *Gymnasien* have the best trained minds. Give me a student who has been taught his Latin grammar, and I will answer for his chemistry.'"[1] A trained mind is the best preparation for rigorous science, and the study of Latin grammar trains the mind. Modernity likes to treat words as though they were a warm bath; the study of Latin enables the student to use words with the precision of a surgeon's scalpel.

Moreover, students of Latin are culturally literate, and have a good sense of how one culture will grow out of others—with traces of the previous cultures everywhere. This can be seen in the stories behind words like *narcissism* or *hermaphrodite*, the history of the office of senator, the meaning

---

[1] Kelsey, *Latin and Greek in American Education* (New York, NY: Macmillan, 1911), p. 24.

of dollar signs, architecture, constellations, wedding customs, and, of course, *et cetera*. Latin students have a better grasp of the history of our culture, and of our cultural identity over the long run. They are less likely to make the common mistake of confusing rivers with ponds. The "90's" are not a self-contained pond, but rather part of a long and interesting cultural river. And what happened "upstream" eighteen hundred years ago *matters*.

The aesthetic considerations are great as well. Classical literature is opened to the student in a wonderful way. A doorway is opened to ancient classical literature—*i.e.*, Virgil, *et al.* Latin also helps with appreciation of English literature, because great English literature was written by men and women steeped in the classics. Their work is filled with classical references and allusions, through which the uneducated modern reader is either bewildered or bypassed.

This benefit is not just limited to a passive appreciation of what *others* have done. Part of the reason for teaching these things is so that our children will come to understand how to express their faith in Christ in an effective way. What aesthetic good is the study of Latin? When students understand, great writing, in other languages and their own, this is a wonderful preparation for those students who have been gifted with writing ability themselves. Genius, like everything else in this fallen world, must be *cultivated* to grow to its potential. It is true that an intelligent child could possibly teach himself to read by staring at cereal boxes. And he may have enough natural ability to learn to write well. But what would the result have been if same child had been studying the *Aeneid* instead? Although we are engaged in a cultural war, few of the Christian participants have seen the importance of equipping our children with *cultural* weapons. "But before men can write this way, they must be educated to do so. We should long for the day when believing Christians no longer write letters to the editor with fisted crayons, when we no longer debate with wooly minds and brick tongues. We should ache for believers who are capable of presenting the truths of the faith in magnificent language . . ."[2] But this will not happen apart from a return to a *classical* education.

Biblical studies also receive a great benefit from Latin as well. For the average believer, classical studies help provide the necessary background for the context of the New Testament. Examples are legion. Castor and Pollux were the Gemini twins mentioned in Acts 28:11. They are still with us today whenever someone uses the expression *jiminy*, which comes from Gemini. Saul and Barnabas were mistaken for Zeus and Hermes in Acts 14:12. An awareness of this will prevent a finicky counterfeit holiness that sometimes plagues the church today. *Epaphroditus* (Phil.2:25; 4:18) had a name which said he was dedicated to Aphrodite, the goddess of sexual love. *Tychicus* (Acts 20:4) means "fateful," after Tyche, the child of Zeus. Along the same line, *Eutychus* (Acts 20:9) means "fortunate" or "good fate." *Syntyche* (Phil. 4:2) means "with fate." The origin of *Fortunatus* (1 Cor. 16:17) is obvious. *Hermes* (Rom. 16:14) meant "herald of the gods." His Roman name was Mercury. Because he was the god of messages, we get the name of the science of interpretation—*hermeneutics*—from him. *Demetrius* (3 John 12) is one who "belongs to Ceres," the goddess of grain. Her name is with us today in the word *cereal*. *Dionysius* (Acts 17:34) is one who is devoted to Bacchus, the god of wine and drunkenness. And *Apollos* (Acts 18:24) is one who was "given by Apollo," the god of the sun. The names of many of the saints in the New Testament are related to a pagan worldview. The fact that early Christians did not change their names may give new significance to Paul's injunction, "Give no offense . . . to the Greeks" (1 Cor. 10:32).

We are told in 2 Peter 2:4 that God threw disobedient angels into *Tartarus*—what is that? A student of the classical world would understand it to be the deepest pit of Hades.

---

[2] Roy Atwood & Douglas Wilson, *A Quest for Authentic Higher Education* (Moscow, ID: Canon Press, 1996), p. 28.

Okay, so what is *that*? In Acts 16:16, Paul cast a demon out of a girl who was a devotee of the god Apollo. We know this because she had "the spirit of a python." The python was sacred to the god Apollo, and was associated with the Oracle at Delphi. Simply put, the background of the New Testament is incomprehensible without a knowledge of classical Greek and Latin antiquity. This means that a good understanding of the New Testament will be extraordinarily difficult without some knowledge of this background.

Obviously, this is even more important for those young men who grow up and are called to the Christian ministry. For the future minister, classical studies provide the same background which all Christians would be blessed to have, but which teachers of the Word *must* have. R.L. Dabney makes the point this way: "But ought not the modern pastor to possess this minimum qualification? Should he not be abreast, at least, of the Ephesian mechanic?. . . the events, the history, the geography, the usages, the modes of thought, the opinions, which constituted the human environment of the New Testament writers, the accurate understanding of which is so necessary to grasp the real scope of what they wrote, all these were the familiar, popular, contemporaneous knowledge of that intelligent mechanic in Ephesus."[3] A familiarity with the classical world is a familiarity with the world into which Christ was born, and is a tremendous preparation for the ministry of the Word.

Some may be convinced, but wonder why Christians should start with Latin instead of Greek. The study of one of these languages is central to the idea of a classical education, but which should you undertake to learn and teach first? The answer is—it depends. If you are starting from scratch, Latin is easier, and provides a good stepping stone to the study of Greek. With Latin you do not have to learn a new alphabet,

---

[3] R. L Dabney, "A Thoroughly Educated Ministry," in *Discussions, Evangelical* (Harrisonburg, VA: Sprinkle Pub., 1982), p. 664.

and the meaning of mar.y of the words is immediately obvious. As mentioned above, about half of our English vocabulary comes from Latin. This is really encouraging for young students in learning Latin vocabulary. For example, *agricola* is *farmer*, *femina* is *woman*, *tuba* is *trumpet*, *villa* is *farmhouse*, and so forth. In contrast, the simple Greek word for truth— αληϑέια—can be intimidating for a young student. So Greek is harder, but at the same time many Christians have had some considerable experience in studying Greek already. In other words, you may have a qualified teacher for Greek and not for Latin. If this is the case, you may want to build upon what you have already done, and just start with Greek. In either case, as you teach your children, do not start by teaching them grammatical concepts. Beginning at about the third grade level, just teach them basic vocabulary and to chant the verb and noun endings. Memorization at this age is easy for them, and it will come in handy when you get to the grammatical instruction later. In this way it is also easier for you to learn the language while you are teaching it.

Some may still be unconvinced by the whole "classical thing." They may be worried whether or not Latin is a Trojan Horse, bringing humanism into Christian education. First, notice how the objection is made more plausible through the use of a picture from Homer's *Iliad*. Secondly, we may answer the concern by admitting that it is quite true. Classical education *can* be an occasion for stumbling. But so can any kind of education be such an occasion. Literacy can stumble. So can lack of education, and lack of literacy. If we love God with all our minds, we will be safe wherever we go. If we do not, we will not be safe anywhere. In the meantime, it is our duty to love Him with *all* our minds, and this includes our study of the history of our language, culture, and people.

How To Start

"Latin. Yeah, right." The work involved in providing your students with the education you wish you and your teachers had received can be overwhelming. Even if you are sold on the *idea* of Latin, it is important to avoid discouragement—discouragement now will only guarantee that the teachers in your school fifty years from now will be saying, "Latin. Yeah, right."

At the same time, even if you avoid discouragement, there are practical questions which still have to be answered. And at the top of the list is the very real question of whether it is even possible to have your students learn Latin when no one you know knows any Latin. "How are we supposed to teach a subject we do not know?"

It is a good question—especially when you consider the fact that of all people, those who are interested in providing a *classical* education to their children will be *least* interested in providing them with a slipshod approach to Latin, or with just a smattering of words.

The first thing to settle is the principle. Do you want it to happen or not? And if you want it, how much do you want it? When the board of our school first made the decision to teach Latin at the elementary level, we did so on the basis of educational principle. At the time the decision was made, we had no Latin teacher. But we did know what we wanted, and how much we wanted it. We now have Latin instruction in the third through sixth grade, and again in ninth and tenth. You may surprise yourselves and discover that the recovery of Latin studies is simply difficult, not impossible.

The second thing is for one of the school's founders to consider learning the language in order to get your program off the ground. This is an area where many parents will not be willing to pay good money for you to hand them *porcum in sacco.*[4] But if you are willing to *give* yourself initially to the establishment of a Latin program, there will be many parents who will be happy to cooperate with you. And after you have taught the subject for several years, and the results have

---

[4] A pig in a poke.

begun to speak for themselves, you already have Latin as a cornerstone of your program.

We are in a position to do a decent job in taking the first steps to recover a classical education. But at the same time, do not expect classical scholars to start falling out of the sky tomorrow. We are involved in a task of rebuilding a culture, and in our view the task will take at least several generations. It is important that you not be ashamed of small beginnings, and at the same time you must recognize that they are, in fact, *small* beginnings. This is doubly important because some of your acquaintances will no doubt be thinking, "Teaching Latin? Him? Who does he think *he* is?" So proceed with humility. If you have the good fortune to hire someone who already knows Latin, you will be in a position to build your program much more quickly. But in either case, you will be able to start *building*.

The third thing you must do is choose your materials. There are several different aspects to this. The first aspect is that of gathering a resource library. The best advice I can give here is for you to haunt used bookstores. Many of them have a foreign language section, and the *least* pawed-through part of it could well be the place where some Latin treasures are. One time I obtained *Harper's Latin Dictionary* (approximately 2,000 pages) at a used bookstore for $17.00. In this way, you can pick up old grammars, classics, classics with translation, books on the etymology of words, *etc.* This is an extremely cost-effective use of your time. The second aspect of gathering is to get some standard helps, even if you need to buy them new. For help with this you should look into any decent college library.

A Basic Question—Pronunciation

One of the biggest problems confronting those teachers of Latin who are learning while they teach is the problem of proper pronunciation. Actually, this is a very minor problem, but it does cause a lot of unnecessary but still vexing

turmoil. However in the final analysis "proper" pronunciation is not really a big deal.

Three main schools of pronunciation contend for your
allegiance. The first is the classical, or, rather, what scholars
have given us as an educated approximation of the classical.
Virgil, Cicero and Augustus never actually spoke into a tape
recorder (that we know of), and consequently, the way they
spoke is not really determinatively settled. But even if the
reconstructions of the scholars are entirely accurate, we are
still dealing with a pronunciation used by the *intelligentsia*
during the reign of Augustus. In other words, this was the
pronunciation of a comparative handful of people. There is
no compelling reason why we must endure various linguistic
tortures in order to master it. As we consider the question of
pronunciation, Caesar's great "I came, I saw, I conquered"
will serve well to illustrate the differences. The classical pronunciation of *Veni, vidi, vici* would be *waynee, weedee, weekee.*

Those who have some experience with Latin in church
choirs will probably be familiar with the second pattern—
ecclesiastical or medieval Latin. If you took Latin in a Catholic school, this was probably the pronunciation pattern you
were taught.[5] The pronunciation of Caesar's comment would
be *veeni, veedi, vichi.*

The "Old" or "Protestant" method is the third, and the
simplest—just pronounce it as though it were English. This is
also a traditional method of handling Latin pronunciation,
and it has a great deal to commend it. "This probably began
to be used in this country during the fifteenth century . . .

---

[5] "If you took Latin in a parochial school, you were probably
taught to pronounce the letter 'V' like the English 'V,' the dipthong
'ae' like 'sundae', and Caesar like 'CHAY-sahr.' If you do this, you
are going to take some flak from Latin purists, classics snobs, and
other assorted lingo bores, but on the other hand, you're going to
get a much better table in the Vatican restaurant." Henry Beard,
Latin for All Occasions (New York, NY: Villard Books, 1990), p.
xvii.

chiefly in order to keep the pronunciation of Latin in line with that of the vernacular, which was also changing rapidly at about that period. This harnessing of the Latin to the vernacular is traditional in every country, and has very much to be said for it."[6] Following this procedure, Caesar's boast would be *venee, viddee, vicki*, unless you are from Texas.

So don't worry about it—but for the sake of your students on a day-to-day basis, be consistent. Most Latin work is not concerned with oral proficiency, but rather with written translation. Latin classes are not classes in *conversational* Latin. If you mispronounce Spanish you will draw laughter from the waiter at your table in Madrid. The same is not the case for Latin. Those most likely to be indignant at "mispronounced" Latin are a small band of purists, whose mentality had a lot to do with the killing of Latin as a living language in the first place. As C.S. Lewis put it, speaking of finicky humanist scholars of the sixteenth century, "They succeeded in killing the medieval Latin: but not in keeping alive the schoolroom severities of their restored Augustanism."[7] Again, the benefits of Latin study are not to be found in conversational Latin. The benefits are great, and much more broad.[8]

---

[6] Dorothy Sayers, "The Teaching of Latin: A New Approach" in *The Poetry of Search and the Poetry of Statement* (London: Gollancz, 1963), p. 190.

[7] C.S. Lewis, *English Literature in the Sixteenth Century* (London, Oxford University Press, 1954), p. 21. Dorothy Sayers makes the same point. "But if it is dead today, it is because the Classical Scholars killed it by smothering it with too much love." Sayers, "The Teaching of Latin: A New Approach" in *The Poetry of Search and the Poetry of Statement* (London: Gollancz, 1963), p. 194.

[8] I should acknowledge one area where pronunciation is important, albeit for a limited few. For those students who excel in classical studies in the high school years, and go on to major in classics at college, pronunciation is crucial in learning the meter of Latin poets.

How Latin Works

This is a language of case endings. In English we determine the syntactical function of a word by its placement in the sentence. For example, in *the girl saw the boy*, the word *girl* is the subject and *boy* the direct object. We determine which is which through the word order. If we were to change the order, we change the meaning of the sentence completely. If *boy* were the subject, then it would have to come first.

This is not how Latin works. In Latin, the various syntactical functions of a noun are determined by what are called case endings. Word order does not play the same role in Latin as it does in English. If we take a typical Latin word—*puer*, for boy—we must suit it for the various roles it may play in a sentence by placing different endings on it. Thus, if *boy* were the subject, it would be *puer*. If we were trying to show possession, *i.e.* the *boy's*, the word would have to be *pueri*. If the boy were the indirect object in the sentence, it would show up as *puero*. If the direct object, then *puerum*. And if the boy were accompanying someone somewhere, it would be again *puero*. And so we breathe a sigh of relief. But, wait . . . we forgot the plural forms which have to cover the same territory, and which are *pueri*, *puerorum*, *pueris*, *pueros*, and *pueris*. Thus, the simple word for *boy* can take any one of ten forms.

But wait, there's more. The word for *boy* belongs to a family of nouns which have the same kind of endings, called the Second Declension. However, there are *four* other such families or declensions. This means that, in dealing with nouns, the student has to know fifty different endings. Endings are also important to the understanding of both adjectives and verbs. Adjectives must match the noun they modify in gender, number, and case, which means that the endings learned for the nouns can also show up on the adjectives.

This is why use of the grammar stage of the Trivium is so important in teaching Latin. The task of a teacher of young children is to fill up tender wits with endings of all kinds. For young children, it is very easy for them to learn to chant

their noun endings *a, ae, ae, am, a! ae, arum, is, as, is! us, i, o,*
um, o! i, orum, is, os, is! And so on. This age is also a good time
to fill up their minds with large lists of vocabulary words,
and other sets of endings, primarily those of the verbs. Later,
in the dialectic stage, they start assembling the pieces, learning the grammar. They are beginning to make grammatical
sense of the language. In the rhetoric stage of the Trivium,
they are capable of translation from original sources, and a
beginning appreciation for the language..

Verbs are much more orderly in Latin than in English.
For example, in order to conjugate the verb *praise* in English
in the present tense, I have to sprinkle it with pronouns. The
verb is meaningless by itself unless I say, *I praise, you praise, he
praises, we praise, you praise, they praise.* The word *praise* remains constant except for the third person singular, for reasons best known to itself. But in Latin, all this is accomplished
without pronouns, through the use of simple endings—*o, s, t,
mus, tis, nt.* These endings are attached to the stem, giving us
laudo, laudas, laudat, laudamus, laudatis, laudant. The language
is orderly and precise. While there are interesting exceptions
to various grammatical rules, the Latin language is characterized by *order.* For those who give themselves to learning it,
and teaching it, that study contains tremendous reward.

Obviously, this is nothing more than a bare bones introductory outline. But for those who are convinced that the
teaching of Latin is important, it should demonstrate the basic outline of how the language works. Detailed resources
and materials are readily available. The one thing remaining
is to make that necessary commitment.

TWELVE:

The Why and How of History
Chris Schlect

"Historical study is absolutely necessary for a stalwart Christianity." —J. Gresham Machen[1]

With good reason, Herodotus of Halicarnassus has been called the Marco Polo of antiquity. He spent the better part of his life, some 2,500 years ago, travelling away from his home, a small coastal city on the south-Aegean coast of Asia Minor. He knew the Aegean region well, and probably visited Athens, then in its Golden Age, more than once. He went as far west as Italy; southward, he sailed the Nile clear to Assuan. His eastward travels took him to Babylon and Susa. To the north he sailed the Black Sea and up the rivers that flow into it. He learned of the customs and the past of the peoples he met, and he wrote down what he learned. He cleverly organized this vast amount of material according to the chronology of Persia, the great empire in his day. As he recounted Persia's rise to preeminence, he told about each land she conquered, culminating in Persia's failure to take Greece.

Ancient scribes and librarians copied his writings on papyrus scrolls. When they were rolled, visible on the outside of the papyrus—serving the purpose of titles on our modern-

---

[1] W. John Cook, ed., *The New Testament: Its Literature and History* (Edinburgh: The Banner of Truth Trust, 1976), p. 10.

day book covers—was the following inscription: "Herodotus of Halicarnassus: Researches." Before that time, the Greek word *historia*, here rendered "researches," was a general term that could refer to any inquiry into any matter. But because of Herodotus, its meaning became much more specialized. History, as the *term* came to be understood, was born there: a systematic inquiry into past events and their relations to one another. One lexicographer notes that the meaning added to this term by Herodotus' influence "marks a literary revolution."[2]

Thus Herodotus is deemed "father of history." This title is deserved, for he was among the first who sought to record events the way they actually transpired, and to critically weigh his sources of information. Others would follow in his steps: Thucydides, Xenophon, Polybius, Livy, Tacitus, to name but a few, as well as such great biographers as Suetonius, Diogenes Laertius, and especially Plutarch. What survives from these ancient sources supplies us with most of our knowledge of antiquity, and their writings are among the greatest works of Western literature. From Herodotus' day forward, the value of historical study has been noted by all educated westerners, and history has taken on a fundamental role in education ever since.

Since the Reformation, Protestants have viewed historical study as a discipline that is essential for the church's well being and the success of the Gospel. In the sixteenth century, John Foxe committed his life to preserving the memory of those who suffered on account of the Gospel. His massive *Actes and Monuments* remains one of the church's most precious possessions. In 1700, Cotton Mather completed his ponderous *Magnalia Christi Americana* ("The Great Works of Christ in America") in order to remind his New England countrymen of their covenantal obligations to the God who

---

[2] Croiset, cited in How and Wells, *A Commentary on Herodotus*, (London: Oxford, 1928), Vol. 1, p. 53.

had established them. The introduction to this work is an urgent exhortation to study history, a task which Mather viewed to be of utmost importance. His *Magnalia* is among the best primary sources for studying the New England Puritans. A generation later Jonathan Edwards carefully penned accounts of the revivals he witnessed so that future generations would remember God's work. The nineteenth century witnessed a tremendous flourish of historical study among Protestants, and the work of many Christian scholars of that period remain the best secondary sources of historical knowledge in the church.

Christians today are growing less and less interested in history, doing so despite our Lord's command to preserve the knowledge of what He has done in the past (cf. Deut. 6:20-25; Josh. 4:5-7; 1 Ch. 16:7ff.; Lk. 17:32; etc.). The few historical writings that are published by Christians nowadays are not read widely. A look at the Christian book market reveals that the average churchman today has little interest even in remedial history. How many today can truthfully sing with David, "I remember the days of old; I meditate on all your works; I muse on the work of your hands" (Ps. 143:5)? We need a reminder of history's importance, and the prominent role it ought to have in the Christian curriculum.

The Classical Historians on History

In their large published works, most classical historians explain, often in prefatory comments, why they have undertaken their study. The historians of classical antiquity thought it their duty to do so, for any true scholar should demonstrate that his subject deserves study. Christian historians, far more than others, ought to know the importance of history. Given that our Lord judges those who waste time on vain pursuits, we had better be assured that history is worthwhile. In addition to Christian obedience, knowing the importance of one's work carries the practical benefit of keeping both the worker motivated and his work focussed. And as one's understanding of his subject's importance grows, his efforts will be better directed.

So why is the study of history important? Naturally, Scripture provides the reasons. And by God's grace, classical historians came to understand many of these reasons in spite of their ungodliness. With Scripture as our guide, then, we may learn the importance of historical study from many of these ancient scholars. After considering them, we will move on to the foundation—the testimony of Scripture.

Some may be tempted to weigh their own personal experience as sufficient training for life, finding little value in historical study. But if experience is a teacher (and indeed it is), history must be even more valuable. In the preface to his magnificent *Library of History* (completed c. 49 B.C.), Diodorus of Sicily explains why this is so. Those who compose histories, he says, help human society as a whole, "for by offering a schooling, which entails no danger, in what is advantageous they provide their readers, through such a presentation of events, with a most excellent kind of experience." The experience offered by history is excellent because it is painless to the student. Diodorus continues:

> For although the learning which is acquired by experience in each separate case, with all the attendant toils and dangers, does indeed enable a man to discern in each instance where utility lies, . . . yet the understanding of the failures and successes of other men, which is acquired by the study of history, affords a schooling that is free from actual experience of ills. . . . For it is an excellent thing to be able to use the ignorant mistakes of others as warning examples for the correction of error, and, when we confront the varied vicissitudes of life, instead of having to investigate what is being done now, to be able to imitate the successes which have been achieved in the past. Certainly all men prefer in their counsels the oldest men to those who are younger, because of the experience which has accrued to the former through the lapse of time; but it is a fact that such experi-

ence is in so far surpassed by the understanding which is gained from history, as history excels, we know, in the multitude of facts at its disposal. For this reason one may hold that the acquisition of a knowledge of history is of the greatest utility for every conceivable circumstance of life . . . (I.1.i-v)[3]

Diodorus' *a fortiori* argument for the study of history is irrefutable. If learning comes through experience, then how much more does it come through the study of history! For history draws from far more numerous and varied experiences than one individual could ever attain in a lifetime, and this experience brings no bitter consequences to the student. Polybius (c. 208-126 B.C.) had said in this same connection, "the surest and indeed the only method of learning how to bear bravely the vicissitudes of fortune, is to recall the calamities of others" (I.1.ii).[4]

A second reason for history's importance is found in the analysis of Thucydides, who stands alongside Herodotus as the greatest of historians. When war broke out between Athens and Sparta in 431 B.C. he resolved to record what transpired. While acknowledging man's natural tendency to regard contemporary events as having utmost historical import, he notes that "this war will prove, for men who judge from the actual facts, to have been more important than any that went before" (I.21).[5] He then weighs the Peloponnesian War against the great wars that had preceded his own day, espe-

---

[3] Diodorus, *Library of History*, C.H. Oldfather, trans. (Cambridge: Harvard University Press; Loeb Classical Library, 1933), pp. 5, 7.

[4] Polybius, *The Histories of Polybius*, W.R. Paton, trans. (Cambridge: Harvard University Press; Loeb Classical Library, 1928), Vol. 1, p. 3.

[5] Thucydides, *History of the Peloponnesian War*, Charles Forster Smith, trans. (Cambridge: Harvard University Press; Loeb Classical Library, 1928), Vol. 1, p. 39.

cially the Trojan War and the Persian Wars. Thucydides was so convinced of the Peloponnesian War's importance that he predicted that it would remain so to future generations. His reason for this is insightful, and it suggests something about the value of historical study. He writes,

> [W]hosoever shall wish to have a clear view both of the events which have happened and of those which will some day, in all human probability, happen again in the same or a similar way for these to adjudge my history profitable will be enough for me. And, indeed, it has been composed, not as a prize-essay to be heard for the moment, but as a possession for all time. (I.22)[6]

Here, Thucydides holds his own work up to one of the great rules of history: similar events happen again and again. Or put more famously, history repeats itself. This is why we can learn from the past. For the circumstances we face today, and will face in the future, will resemble those that others have encountered before. Thus, the extent to which a historian's work is a "possession for all time" depends upon how closely the events it covers relate to experiences which all men share. Indeed, the Peloponnesian War is quite remote to us in both time and geography. But Thucydides' narrative of that war brilliantly depicts matters that all peoples face throughout time: the science of statecraft, along with the intricacies of alliances and diplomacy; the psychology of a people at war; a theatre-wide analysis of war strategy; the political and strategic impact of fighting either on home or foreign soil; the assets and drawbacks of different types of leadership; the frailty of peace; and the list could go on. Those who have studied any of the great conflicts of modernity, from the Napoleonic Wars through Vietnam or the Cold War, will be thunderstruck by Thucydides' continuing relevance. Understanding that history repeats itself, he extracted the timeless elements from

---

[6] *Ibid.*, p. 41.

his own era and used them to teach us about our world today, just as he has taught men for the last 2,500 years. Outside Scripture, there exist few better studies of corporate human nature than Thucydides' *History of the Peloponnesian War*.

Thucydides articulates, and embodies, one very important reason to study history. Simply put, history is relevant.
This is so because the past resembles the present and future,
for no circumstance exists but that which is common to man.
This observation also suggests a criterion for good historical
study, being the sort that sheds light on the present and future.

Livy (59 B.C. to A.D. 17) devoted forty years of his life
to the composition of his monumental history of Rome. His
introduction to the 142-book masterpiece includes the following remark in praise of history which, perhaps better than
any other, offers a fitting conclusion to our discussion of the
wisdom of the ancients on the value of historical study. The
ancients saw history to be important for two reasons: first,
because it draws from a wide range of human experience that
is gained without toil; and second, because that experience
bears upon matters that all men face. Livy writes,

> The study of history is the best medicine for a sick mind;
> for in history you have a record of the infinite variety of
> human experience plainly set out for all to see; and in that
> record you can find for yourself and your country both
> examples and warnings; fine things to take as models, base
> things, rotten through and through, to avoid. (I.1.x)[7]

The Basis of Historical Study

The historians of classical antiquity were much less successful in accounting for these tremendous benefits of history
than they were in pointing them out. They knew well that
history is very useful, as we have seen. But Christians will

---

[7] Livy, *The Early History of Rome*, Aubrey de Selincourt, trans.
(London: Penguin, 1971), p. 34.

not be surprised to find that they couldn't really explain why. Diodorus offered the best self-conscious attempt. He made bold to consider the philosophical underpinnings of history by addressing the critical question, "How is it that past events correspond to the present and future?" He sought recourse in the Stoic doctrine of the universal kinship of man.

> . . . it has been the aspiration of these writers [i.e., historians] to marshal all men, who, although united one to another by their kinship, are yet separated by space and time, into one and the same orderly body. And such historians have therein shown themselves to be, as it were, ministers of Divine Providence. For just as Providence, having brought the orderly arrangement of the visible stars and the natures of men together into one common relationship, continually directs their courses through all eternity, apportioning to each that which falls to it by direction of fate, so likewise historians, in recording the common affairs of the inhabited world as though they were those of a single state, have made of their treatises a single reckoning of past events and a common clearinghouse of knowledge concerning them. (I.1.iii-iv)[8]

To a Stoic, Divine Providence is a vague pantheistic force, and human kinship is grounded in man's participation in this force. Christian apologists can easily reduce ancient Stoic pantheism to absurdity. Yet there remains much to be appreciated in Diodorus' thought even from a Christian standpoint. First, he rightly observes that historical study presupposes regularity over time in the affairs of men. If a genuinely novel circumstance entered the course of human events, history could not inform us about how to deal with it. Second, he correctly acknowledges that all men, in all times and cultures, share an essentially common nature. Historical study also presupposes this to be true, for if contemporary man bears

---

[8] Diodorus, *Library of History*, Vol. 1, pp. 6-8.

no relation to men of the past, then the lessons of the past have no application today.

While Diodorus insightfully identifies the two basic presuppositions of historical study, his Stoicism fails to account for them. For pantheism cannot produce a coherent and knowable principle of order from its commitment to the absolute diversity of nature. But if Divine Providence is understood as it should be—as the personal governance of the triune God over all creation, and if human kinship is grounded in man's unique status as God's image-bearer, then what Diodorus had said would be quite accurate. In Christ, not in a pantheistic force, all creation coheres (Col. 1:17). God's governance over His creation in Christ provides the regularity over time that is presupposed in historical study (cf. Gen. 8:22). Our connection to other men, even those in other times and places—also presupposed in historical study—is similarly grounded in God's design for man. Paul introduced both these points to Athenian philosophers, some of them Stoics, saying, "God, who made the world and everything in it . . . gives to all life, breath, and all things. And he has made from one blood every nation of men to dwell on all the face of the earth, and has determined their preappointed times and the boundaries of their habitation" (Acts 17:24-26).

This God, the triune God of Scripture who has made Himself known in the person of Jesus Christ, is the God of human history. J.H. Merle D'Aubigne prefaced his multivolume masterpiece, *History of the Reformation* (1835), with a profound declaration on this point:

> History should live by that life which belongs to it, and that life is God. In history God should be acknowledged and proclaimed. The history of the world should be set forth as the annals of the government of the sovereign King.[9]

---

[9] J. H. Merle D'Aubigne, *History of the Reformation* (New York: American Tract Society, 1835) Vol. 1, p. 21.

Only when history is understood this way is it worthwhile and intelligible. Even with all their genius and well-deserved influence, the classical historians failed to grasp history's most essential feature. Another great church historian, Philip Schaff, summarizes the point very well in his *History of the Christian Church*: "The idea of universal history presupposes the idea of the unity of God, and the unity and common destiny of men, and was unknown to ancient Greece and Rome."[10]

The Significance of History

From a Christian standpoint, the importance of understanding history is inestimable. Our faith rests on history, particularly on the ministry of Christ in history. Writing during the reign of Trajan, a century after Christ, the great historian Tacitus mentions "Christus" who had "undergone the death penalty in the reign of Tiberius, by sentence of the procurator Pontius Pilatus."[11] But we believe that Christ died for a better reason than that Tacitus tells us so. We believe the testimony of Scripture, the only infallible record of history. There we not only read that Christ died, but that he did so for our sins (1 Cor. 15:3), and that He also rose on the third day for our justification (Rom. 4:25). If this is not true *historically*, then our faith is vain (1 Cor. 15:14). Thus, the Gospel, the most basic distinctive of Christianity, is at root an historical matter.

Some have attempted to strip history from the Gospel. They have said that the core of our faith is an ever-present relationship with God, or a decision made here and now. Neo-orthodoxy teaches that the Christ of Calvary is transhistorical, a nebulous entity that is out of reach and yet everpresent. Such misconceptions made lasting inroads into main-

---

[10] Philip Schaff, *History of the Christian Church* (Grand Rapids, MI: Eerdmans, [1910] 1991), Vol. 1, p. 2.

[11] Tacitus, *Annals XV.44*, John Jackson, trans. (Cambridge: Harvard University Press; Loeb Classical Library, 1937), Vol. 5, p. 283.

stream Christianity around the turn of the 20th century, and among the apologists who saw the problem clearly was J. Gresham Machen, a true Christian and a true classicist. He forcefully contended that "a gospel independent of history is a contradiction in terms."[12] Machen's opponents claimed then, as many still do, that true religion is grounded not in the Jesus of objective history, but in a subjective Jesus within the Christian himself. Scripture is thusly reduced to being, at most, a moral handbook or a talisman used to awaken the reader's sentimentality. The historicity of its claims become perilously devalued. Machen rightly saw this as an attack upon the heart of the Christian faith. "We Christians are interested not merely in what God commands," he wrote, "but also in what God did; the Christian religion is couched not merely in the imperative mood, but also in a triumphant indicative; our salvation depends squarely upon history; the Bible contains that history, and unless that history is true the authority of the Bible is gone and we who have put our trust in the Bible are without hope."[13]

For Christians, history is important primarily because Christianity is based upon historical events. This sets Christianity apart from most other philosophies. Again, Machen:

> The student of the New Testament should be primarily an historian. The centre and core of all Bible is history. Everything else that the Bible contains is fitted into an historical framework that leads up to an historical climax. The Bible is primarily a record of events.[14]

In addition to the Gospel itself, Christianity advances

---

[12] J. Gresham Machen, *Christianity and Liberalism* (Grand Rapids, MI: Eerdmans, 1923), p. 121.

[13] J. Gresham Machen, *The Virgin Birth of Christ* (New York, NY: Harper & Row, 1930), p. 385.

[14] "History and Faith" in *What is Christianity?*, Ned Stonehouse, ed. (Grand Rapids, MI: Eerdmans, 1951), p. 170.

other important historical claims. We might begin at creation, the historical veracity of which must be upheld to retain the integrity of the entire Christian worldview (Col. 1-2). Also, God created the rainbow to be a concrete history lesson, a reminder of His covenant with Noah and with all the flesh of the earth (Gen. 9:12-17). Likewise, the Passover celebration was a required observance for the Israelites—a God-ordained history lesson about Israel's redemption from bondage in Egypt (Ex. 12). Jesus instituted the Passover of the New Covenant in the same way, charging His disciples to "do this in remembrance of me" (Luke 22:19). In celebrating the Lord's supper, like the Passover of the Old Covenant, we are commanded to remember historical truth—in this case, the breaking of our Lord's body and the spilling of His blood. Both the Old and New institutions of the Passover are, among other things, history lessons.

Heinous sins are traced to a neglect of historical knowledge. Asaph reminds us that the faithless children of Ephraim turned back in the day of battle, for "they refused to walk in His law, and forgot His works and His wonders that He had shown them" (Ps. 78:9-11). They sinned because they forgot what God had done—they forgot history.

In the same Psalm, Asaph exhorts fathers to instruct their children about God's character as it is displayed in history: "telling to the generation to come the praises of the Lord, and His strength and His wonderful works that He has done" (v. 4). Why must fathers do this? That their children would in turn declare the same lesson to the following generation, "that they may set their hope in God, and not forget the works of God, but keep His commandments (v. 7). Note that keeping God's commandments is set here in direct contrast to forgetting the works of God, which are recorded in the annals of history. Christians therefore have a duty both to learn and to teach history.

As a case in point, we may note the Israelites of Jeroboam's time. As part of his scheme to accede the throne of Israel, he convinced the people to neglect their duty to worship Yahweh, and bow to idols instead. Had the people remembered their history, they would never have bowed down to Jeroboam's gold calves. They would have known better when he made this patently false historical claim: "Here are your gods, O Israel, which brought you up from the land of Egypt" (1 Kings 12:28). Not knowing their history, the Israelites were duped by a revisionist. We must raise our children to avoid the sin that ensnared Israel in Jeroboam's time.

The History Curriculum

In heeding the charge to study history, we must first consider what history to study. Do we focus upon ancient history? economic history? the history of labor unions? the history of art? of Christian doctrine? of rock music of the 60's? Actually, all such history is important and worth a Christian's attention. But some types of history are more basic than others and should be deemed essential for an adequate education, whereas others might be set aside for the specialist. Most anything that exists has a history, so naturally, not all histories could be addressed here. Just a few will be considered, and those only at a theoretical level.

Recently, there has been a trend to place great emphasis on modern history. Many textbooks that supposedly survey world or western history may have a paragraph on Julius Caesar, a very brief (if any) mention of Pericles, and two extensive chapters on the Second World War. Theodosius I, who made Christianity the official religion of the Roman Empire, lived about midway between the Trojan War and our day. But if he is mentioned in a text at all, we surely will not find him anywhere close to the middle of the textbook. Almost certainly he would be found in one of opening chapters. This curricular fad of playing up more recent history at the expense of the "ancient" world is truly regrettable, as we shall see. Secularists defend this emphasis on the grounds that modernity is more relevent, a claim which assumes an evolu-

tionary view of human society. But Christians know that
neither human nature nor God's ways have changed through
the ages. Of course, God's kingdom has advanced, and continues to do so as we move along toward the day when his
last enemies are defeated (*cf.* 1 Cor. 15:22-26). But this consideration does not entail the conclusion that the most recent
development in God's plan is the most significant to us simply because it is most recent.

Teachers should focus on those periods of history that
have been especially momentous in God's plan. Of course,
most central is the period surrounding the ministry of Christ.
The political, social, and intellectual history of Rome around
the turn of the millennium is therefore obviously important.
Hellenic and hellenistic studies will provide the context for
this era. Similarly, the recovery of the Gospel during the
Reformation, and the concurrent humanism of the Renaissance, both of which have left an indelible impact upon the
course of human affairs, should receive special treatment. The
influence of thinkers like Plato, Aristotle, Augustine, Calvin,
and Kant cannot be overstated. Secular histories do not give
due attention to developments in church history that Christians know to be very important, such as the persecutions
and doctrinal controversies of the early church, the papacies
of Gregory I, Gregory VII, Boniface VIII, church councils,
and other like matters.

Provincial history is also important, but note that its
importance is of a different sort than that of the events mentioned in the previous paragraph. Provincial history sets the
issues of one's own day in their rightful context. But the issues of our day, in our locale, will be far less significant to
future generations or to people living elsewhere. Provincial
history reviews the events of the recent past going back a few
generations, and local history. For example, a child growing
up in Texas should learn the history of Texas; those in the
United States should study U.S. History, *etc.*

Whether economic, aesthetic, political, intellectual, or

social history is more important depends upon which of these arenas holds the greater sway at a given time. Given that all these arenas are interrelated, this can be difficult to determine. Traditionally, political history is given the most attention, but recent trends in curriculum have helped to bring more recognition to other areas. The kings and the wars of the Renaissance were not nearly as noteworthy as Raphael, Michelangelo, or Brunneleschi. While the Congress of Vienna changed Europe's political landscape, its impact was hard to see even a century later. But at the same time as the Congress convened, one Viennese resident was changing the world forever. Beethoven's music, especially his symphonies, may one day prove to have the most profound, lasting impact of any nineteenth-century events.

While teachers must decide what to teach, they must also determine how to teach it. Remember, the goal is to impart the tools of learning history in order to equip the student to one day venture out on his own and study the subject. They must be taught to interact with primary sources, and to critically evaluate how historical writers treat their sources. These are the tools of historical learning. It makes little sense to learn about Julius Caesar from a book published last year when there is such a wealth of ancient testimony about him.

Studying history should be an important pursuit of God's people. We are commanded to learn and teach history for His glory. Faithful instruction in history will be blessed by the wisdom gained from the lessons of past men's experiences. Christian schools should be centers of historical learning, where the next generation comes to understand the great works that God has done, that they may learn to praise Him for His perfect governance over the affairs of men, and teach future generations to do the same.

THIRTEEN:

The Why and How of Literature
Douglas Wilson

The Return to Classical Standards
A common confusion afflicts those who confront the problems caused by "relaxed standards." In our calling and vocation as educators, these relaxed standards are of course academic standards, but the same problem can readily be seen in every area of life. As standards fall, there will always be a certain number of people who are distressed by it all. They would like to raise the standard; they would like to "tighten up," but they are afraid that "others" will not tolerate it. The mess is the way it now "has to be." Part of the reason we assume others will not accept a return to rigor is that we interpret any amount of resistance as evidence of an upcoming fight to the death. This is nothing less than a failure of nerve on our part.

We assume that a return to standards will provoke some sort of mass revolt, and that we will lose what little influence we have remaining. But as we consider the secular educational world, chasing first after this reform and then after that one, we should recognize that our culture is beginning to develop an ache for the older disciplines in literary nobility and beauty. When that discipline arrives, there will of course be noise and thunder—just as there is a tremendous ruckus when an undisciplined three-year-old finally gets a genuine spanking. But the child needs the discipline, and on a fundamental level wants it, noise notwithstanding.

In the midst of our educational morass, we are seeking to raise the standard of classical Christian excellence in education. Now the phrase "excellence in education" is hackneyed, and it is certainly overdone by the enemies of excellence as they parade their wares. But we must not abandon the genuine in order to show our disapproval of the counterfeit. Just because the current government education fraud talks about excellence does not mean we should react and call for a "return to the lousy."

So what does genuine excellence mean? Prior to any given curriculum choices, it refers first to an attitude—the attitude of the classical mind. We decide, before we begin, that we will *not* tailor our curriculum to suit the student; rather, we educate the student so that he conforms to, and masters, the curriculum. The process of education is larger than we are, and it transcends the generations currently alive. We do not set the pace according to the whims of a sullen kid muttering in the back row. The pace is being called by Homer and Jeremiah, Virgil and Athanasius, Shakespeare and Bunyan, Van Til and Lewis. And as this list should indicate, excellence in education means in good measure a *literary* education. It may not seem very practical, but when we are done we may understand why Lewis commented: "You see at once that education is essentially for freemen and vocational training for slaves."[1]

Will modern kids put up with this? Will their parents? Of course they will—they will embrace the opportunity to work with educators who have the courage of their convictions. If we recognize the opportunity we have, our schools are going to see remarkable growth. If we seek growth through compromising our standards, we may still grow, but the same way a cancer does. But if we stand firm, we will see great blessing. Again, as C.S. Lewis put it, "The only people who

---

[1] C.S. Lewis, *The Quotable Lewis* (Wheaton, IL: Tyndale House, 1989), p. 181.

achieve much are those who want knowledge so badly that they seek it while the conditions are still unfavorable. Favourable conditions never come."[2] Those who recognize this *make* their own favorable conditions. In order to make these conditions, one of the first things which we must do is realize that teaching the aesthetic appreciation of good literature is not an "option," an elective, off to the side for those who like that sort of thing; rather, it is a central part of all true *education*.[3] It may not be necessary to vocational training, but it is central to classical education.

Christians have frequently made an uneasy truce with literature. This is because the teaching of literature presents the Christian educator with quite a problem. On one side he sees a number of well-written books without God and without hope in the world, and on the other he sees evangelical and wholesome fluff. Sometimes teachers who care about literature must feel as though they are being forced to choose between serving food prepared by a world-renowned chef, who persists in poisoning the meals, and a steady diet of *Twinkies* prepared by born-again factory workers. Is there another option?

Parents who want their children to receive a classical education will be reluctant to direct them a course of sappy books, whether or not the authors are Christians. And parents who want their children to go to heaven when they die will be reluctant to turn them over to a course of reading produced by erudite and eloquent God-haters. The problem is compounded by the fact that, unlike the government schools, private schools excel in teaching their students to *read*. And once the children learn to read, they roar through all the good books available, and a major problem then presents itself.

---

[2] C. S. Lewis, *The Weight of Glory* (Grand Rapids, MI: Eerdmans, 1965), p. 52.

[3] "There is nothing in literature which does not, in some degree, percolate into life." C.S. Lewis, *The Allegory of Love* (Oxford: Oxford University Press, 1936), p. 130.

What do we do *now?* Our kids are all dressed up with no place to go.

But before embarking on the quest for the "perfect book list," it is important to master certain principles *first*. Otherwise, your students' reading is more likely to be based on whims and fads and the "latest rage" than upon sturdy biblical principle. And of course, by "sturdy biblical principle" I do *not* mean a book in which everyone gets saved in the last chapter, and the heroine marries the fellow who was so tall, dark, and godly. "Quite an answer to prayer, really."

The problem with such books is that the sentimentalism contained in them is nothing more than the idiot child of the Romantic Movement, which was a full-scale rebellion against the God of the Bible. Sentimentalist drivel is simply a continuation of this same revolt, even if it *is* conducted far less competently. Sentimentalism in writing is nothing more than pornography for the emotions.

The first thing to realize is that biblical thinking and captivating writing are not antithetical concepts. The fact that the combination is so rare in our contemporary culture is simply a testimony to the retreatist mentality that has afflicted evangelical Christians since the general cultural apostasy of the last century. As believing Christians, our desire should be to do *everything* we do to the glory of God. This means we should not write, and we should not read, Christian books which are a bunch of nothing. A Christian literature program is not one in which the students read "Christian books." A Christian literature program is one in which the students are taught to read great literature, and to *think* while they read, as Christians. As they do, our children must be taught to appreciate a finely-crafted sentence—to the glory of God. As Christians, we are people of the Word, and consequently, we should be people of *words*. We should understand words and use them well.

The second principle we must understand is that biblical faith is not moralism. What many mean by *Christian* books

is simply *decent* books—some kids' story with Disneyfied standards. But this sort of thing is rarely Christian; it is simply G-
rated paganism. When this principle is not understood, many
parents are tempted to rate books according to some very
simple *shibboleth—i.e.* "Does it have swear words in it?" The
problem of course is that some utterly humanistic books meet
such standards, and some wonderful Christian books do not.
Also related to this is the fact that our modern moralism is
detached from biblical moorings, and is consequently determined by the latest rage in contemporary "ethics"—whether
political correctness, self-esteem, feminism, or whatnot. This
results in the reader being confronted with the spectacle of a
King Arthur, say, working through his problems with low
self-esteem.

The third principle is that if your children are being educated to think like Christians to the glory of God, they should
be equipped to read and analyze, and to a certain extent, appreciate, the writing of godless writers who were, nevertheless, craftsmen. One can appreciate some of Twain's writing,
for example, while understanding his despair and refusing to
follow him in it.

The temptation is, once the children have learned to read,
to turn them over to the books. But this is abdication, and
not *teaching*. Christian teachers should not use books the way
many government school teachers use video—as a cheap
babysitter and no-brainer. Parents, and the teachers they hire,
are responsible for what is going into their children's minds—
it does not matter if the source is television, the neighbors'
kids, or the books checked out of the school library. But in
order to avoid such abdication, parents and teachers must be
diligent readers as well, and they should have a good idea of
how books are shaping both their children's worldview, and
this includes their understanding and appreciation of well-
written literature.

At the same time, we must recognize that books are not
to be viewed *simply as entertainment* (an erroneous view in-

troduced to us by Edgar Allen Poe, who rejected any didactic or teaching role for literature). Because we think that we are reading this or that to be entertained, and because when we are being entertained we want to relax, and, as Christians, in order to relax, the author and book must be "safe," we therefore want a list of books which contains nothing troubling, controversial, or problematic. Thus, the desire for a safe evangelical *Index* of books is itself something we have gotten from the world. It is not a Christian sentiment at all; *it is worldly.* There is therefore a difference between recommending books to read and discuss and *think through* on the one hand, and endorsing such books along with anything they might contain on the other. As we think through such issues, it is important for us to demonstrate to our children how our reading habits should be shaped and molded to the glory of God.

Literature and the Culture War
The great temptation is to answer the general deterioration of our culture with nothing other than high-octane theology and apologetics. Those small bands of Christians who see what is going on around us are tempted constantly to explain to others, bluntly and plainly, what they see. *Don't you understand?* And when they turn to the work of education, they want to graduate epistemological Navy Seals, who are all ready to board the choppers, leave the carrier Reformation, and head out on the mission *now.*

This thinking is understandable of course. Truth in our age is so neglected, and that same truth is so important, that we think we have no time to varnish it. Just set it out there, and if the God-haters don't like it, well, let them learn to cope. While this has a certain appeal, the problem is that the unvarnished truth is not really the truth. In a fallen world, truth cannot go out unadorned and remain what it is. "Naphtali is a deer let loose; he uses *beautiful* words" (Gen. 49:21). When truth is spoken apart from beauty, it is not really the truth anymore. "Let your speech always be with grace, seasoned with salt, that you may know how you ought to answer each one" (Col. 4:6). Our words are to be lovely, seasoned with salt, suited and adapted to each occasion—a believing application of Aristotle's definition of rhetoric. Shelley was consequently speaking more wisely than he knew when he said that poets are the unacknowledged legislators of the world. We mobilize to restore decency to America through legislation, and when we are done all we have are a bunch of laws, and many times not even that. In contrast, poets and writers shape the minds of generations—whether for good and ill. But here we prove ourselves to be virtually without letters. We, the people of the Word, ought to be masters of words; Christians ought to be preeminent in wordsmithing. We are not. In this hour of crisis, we produce and sell mountains of smarmy goo and oceans of treacle. We wouldn't know a great book if it ran naked through the CBA convention.

Of course the mindless relativism of the secular literary community shows us what creativity and letters will do without the ballast of truth. That is plain enough. But the aesthetic stupidity displayed in the modern evangelical world also shows us what ballast does without a ship. Christian schools which cannot produce great writers are failures as schools.

A great need therefore exists for an uncompromised Christian liberal arts course of study up through the college level. By "uncompromised" we must mean that a thorough understanding of the biblical antithesis must permeate the course of study. Great literature is not to be studied and written because "other things" are just as important as biblical truth, or because it is important in its own autonomous realm. Rather, it is because the truth is so important it must go *everywhere*. Students must be trained to think like Christians everywhere they go, and in everything they read. When they are trained to think in terms of the biblical antithesis, they are then (and only then) equipped to plunder and use the gold of the Egyptians. As T.S. Eliot stated it, "So long as we are conscious of the gulf fixed between ourselves and the greater part of contemporary literature, we are more or less protected from being harmed by it, and are in a position to extract from it what good it has to offer us."[4] But without this antithesis fixed firmly in our minds, we will be seduced as we turn to literature. So why not train the students "in the antithesis," and have them stay away from that bawdy house? Why should we have students study Homer, and Virgil, and Milton, and Shakespeare? Why not just stick to Scripture? The simple answer is that those who "stick to" Scripture have misunderstood it. Scripture requires us to take every thought captive. When we read nothing but Scripture we are refusing to imitate the pattern set for us in Scripture. When the apostle Paul gave his testimony, he quoted from *Agamemnon*, a play by the pagan Aeschylus. It was hard for him to kick against the goads; it is equally hard for those who want to make Scripture a *solitary* book.

The truth is that there is no secular/sacred distinction. "The earth is the Lord's, and all its fulness" (1 Cor. 10:26). Consequently, we cannot protect and preserve any truth by isolating it from the rest of God's world. To do so kills it. The division is not between the secular and the sacred, between theology and literature. The antithesis is between seeing the entire world the way God says to see it, or refusing to see the entire world the way God says to see it. For example, a man who reads but refuses to interpret *The Aeneid* with biblical eyes is disobeying God. The man who refuses to read it at all because he only has time for "theology" and "spiritual things" is doing the same thing—limiting truth to a pietistic ghetto. The outside and impious world is left alone in its rebellion, free to assault the faith at its leisure. C.S. Lewis said it this way. "If you attempted . . . to suspend your whole intel-

---

[4] T.S. Eliot, writing in *The Great Critics* (New York, NY: Norton & Co., 1951), p. 730.

lectual and aesthetic activity, you would only succeed in sub-
stituting a worse cultural life for a better. You are not, in fact,
going to read nothing . . . if you don't read good books you
will read bad ones. If you don't go on thinking rationally,
you will think irrationally. If you reject aesthetic satisfactions
you will fall into sensual satisfactions."[5] And this is precisely
the trap that evangelical pietism has fallen into. Refusing a
cultural life is impossible; all attempts at it will only produce
contemptible and immoral culture. *Pietism must be rejected
by us because it leads directly to impiety.* When the goodness
and greatness of God are well-understood, that understanding will sustain the student everywhere he goes. And he should
be taught to go after a good book.

How To Teach Literature

The foundation of literary appreciation is literacy. It is a great
tragedy that this has to be stated (and, in some quarters, even
argued for), but truisms remain true no matter how many
colleges of education abandon them. One of the most fundamental tasks in all of education is the impartation of literacy—
the ability to read. If this is not done properly, the child will
suffer for it the rest of his life. Consequently, and I apologize
for having to say it, the first step in teaching literature appreciation is to have an elementary program which teaches children how to *read*, and to read *books* from the beginning.

A good school will emphasize literature and good books,
even at the earliest years. There is no reason for making children endure basals when they could be reading good books.
But we must be careful. An emphasis on books is thought by
some to be what is meant by the phrase "whole language." In
reality what is called "the whole language approach" to literacy has been nothing less than a disaster on wheels. But the
confusion is understandable. Whole language instruction en-

---

[5] C.S. Lewis, *The Weight of Glory* (Grand Rapids, MI: Eerdmans,
1949), p. 46.

courages the child to "read for meaning." Whole language encourages an examination of the larger context through reading whole books. Whole language discourages a fixation with the sounds of individual letters, and the meaning of individual words. It deemphasizes "getting at words." It denies objective meaning for words, and places each student in the position of "creating meanings" for the text. In short, whole language is nothing other than deconstructionist literary theory in short pants holding a Barney the dinosaur lunch bucket.

Teaching a child to read properly is not difficult. It has been made difficult by your trained education professionals, and the entire process *has* been shrouded with arcane professional terminology. But there is really only one term that concerned parents need to know and understand, and that is *phonics*. English is a phonetic language. This means, fundamentally, that there is an organized relationship between the letters in each word and the sound of each word. For various reasons, mostly having to do with people like William the Conqueror, this organization in our language is not completely tidy. English is not like Algebra; there are variations and exceptions. Take for example, the word *one*. How on earth do we get the *wuh* sound out of there? Or compare the *ough* in *through, bough, though, cough, rough, etc.* It represents *oo, ow, oh, off,* and *uff* respectively. Remarkable language we have here.

Such phonetic quirks have been used by proponents of whole language as evidence that our children will just be bewildered and bored if we attempt to drill them in the sounds of all the letters. But still, quirks and all, it is possible (and relatively easy) for the average child to memorize the basic phonetic sounds, learn to decode every word from left to right, and then have immediate access to countless written words which he already knows in their spoken form. Put another way, in schools that teach phonics, there are no illiterates coming out of first grade. In the government schools, there are hundreds of thousands of graduates from the twelfth grade who cannot read their own diplomas.

And short of complete illiteracy, there are several other common indicators that a child has been taught badly. One of them is found in that much abused term *dyslexia*. When children are not carefully drilled to make automatic and *careful* distinctions between letters with a similar appearance, say between b and d, or p and q, then they do not make those distinctions. When they continue to confuse such letters on into the upper grades, they can soon find themselves labelled dyslexic, and slapped into a (well-funded) special program. Such students need a special program all right—a well-run first grade classroom, with a teacher who knows how to teach reading.[6]

Such remarkable failures, however, have not caused any significant pedagogical repentance on the part of the education establishment. The culprit behind all of this (the "look-say" method) has now been dressed up in Sunday clothes, surrounded by larger context of real books, and called the whole language approach. The subtlety deceives people. Because our school emphasizes the reading of good books (as opposed to basal readers), our superintendent regularly has to tell people that we do *not* use the whole language approach. There should be no mistake about it; not only is the whole language approach a horrible method of teaching, it is also subtle and deceitful. No one will come to a parent and ask for permission to scramble their children's brains. But that is what happens.

Once a young Christian man, a recent education graduate of a state university, applied to our school for a teaching position. During the board interview, I wanted to check his understanding of the whole language approach which he had been taught, so I asked him what he would do in the following scenario. "Suppose one of your students were shown the letters h-o-r-s-e. Suppose further he read the word aloud as

---

[6] It is time for a revolution. Dyslexics of the world, untie!

pony. What would you say to him?" The young man said that he would praise the student, and tell him he had done a good job. After all, to nitpick about individual letters and words would not be consistent with an emphasis on "whole language." The fact that the young man was a clear Christian had not protected him intellectually from the foolishness he had been taught.

At the root, the whole language approach is simply another part of our rebellious culture's ongoing revolt against objective meaning. This rebellion hates objective meaning because it implies absolutes, and absolutes come from God. Our government schools have required the separation of God and school. The end of this process is the separation of objective meaning and school, or put another way, the separation of education and school. We are not at the end of the road, but we can see it from here.[7]

What Then?

If the whole language approach is staunchly resisted, the result will be students who can read. But literacy, considered in itself, is not an automatic blessing. Literacy can be used to master *TV Guide*, Nintendo instruction manuals, and the *National Enquirer*. Once the student is equipped in reading, he must also be taught to love the lovely. "Finally, brethren, whatever things are true, whatever things are noble, whatever things are just, whatever things are pure, whatever things are lovely, whatever things are of good report, if there is any virtue and if there is anything praiseworthy—meditate on these things" (Phil. 4:8). Lewis put it this way,

---

[7] I was once speaking at a conference and offered some mild criticism of the whole language approach, saying, as I recall, that it was "from the pit." I was talking afterward to a recent graduate of a well-known evangelical Christian college, who was baffled, because "whole language" was being taught there. You can't be too careful.

Literature exists to teach what is useful, to honour what deserves honour, to appreciate what is delightful. The useful, honourable and delightful things are superior to it: it exists for their sake; its own use; honour, or delightfulness is derivative from theirs.[8]

This means that as the students are taught properly, they should grow in their love for great literature. An essential part of this process is having a teacher who loves the literature as well. When a teacher loves and appreciates a book, he is then in a position to teach his students to do the same. Love is contagious.

In addition, the books taught should have met the test of time. This is for two reasons. The first is that when generations have acknowledged the greatness of a work, humility requires that we assume the burden of proof if we want to maintain the contrary. Every reader of great literature will encounter specimens which he thinks ought *not* to have passed the test of time, but humility will dictate that he will assume a deficiency in his own taste, and not in the taste of tens of thousands of his betters. The rest of the army is probably *not* out of step. This does not mean the judgments of our literary ancestors are infallible. We may be right, but we should assume a proper deference. For example, *Paradise Lost* is a great work but not exactly accessible. It would be perilously easy for ill-equipped moderns to dismiss great but difficult literature as poor literature when the deficiencies are in ourselves. At the same time, we must not only resist contemporary trash. If a work is morally degrading, then we must turn away, no matter when it was written. Because our era is ethically bankrupt, more than a few scholars have been excavating ancient literary landfills for evidence that men were wicked then too. Some of the poetry of Catullus has not exactly improved with age.

---

[8] C.S. Lewis, *The Discarded Image* (London: Cambridge University Press, 1964), p. 214.

Further, the teaching of contemporary literature is not really necessary. ". . . [T]he student who wants a tutor's assistance in reading the works of his own contemporaries might as well ask for a nurse's assistance in blowing his own nose."[9] After all, contemporary works were *written* for contemporary readers. Beyond this, contemporary literature is plagued by our modern relativism, the stampedes of faddishness, and the supreme chutzpah of publishing blurbs. For example, the historical novels of Patrick O' Brian, which are decent enough, sport publisher's hype like this on their covers: "the best historical novels ever written." "You will meet nothing like O'Brian in all literature." Whoa. Maybe we should wait and see.

In the third place, books should be studied which are culturally interconnected. When a people share a set monetary currency, it enables them to buy and sell readily—to deal with one another. In the same way, a canon of literature is important for literary understanding and progress. When a disconnected book is read, the blessing resulting from it is self-contained. When the *Iliad* is read and loved, countless other references in countless other books are opened to the reader. He will encounter them everywhere. When the right books are read, each door opens into a hundred rooms. This Western literary canon is hard to miss—Homer, Ovid, Isaiah, Aeneas, Horace, Jeremiah, Aeschylus, Solomon, Sophocles, Chaucer, Shakespeare, Spenser, Dante, Cervantes, Milton, Goethe, Bunyan, Austen, Whitman, and others I have inexplicably failed to mention.[10] The list includes prophets and

---

[9] C.S. Lewis, *The Quotable Lewis* (Wheaton, IL: Tyndale House, 1989), p. 399.

[10] A good background discussion of this canon can be found in Harold Bloom, *The Western Canon* (New York, NY: Harcourt Brace & Company, 1994). His unbelief results in some goofy analysis, and unbelievable exclusions, but nevertheless the book presents a decent lay of the land. Further, the suggested reading list at the end of this section includes a list of books which will serve at least as a beginning.

lunatics, saints like Bunyan and scoundrels like Whitman. Nevertheless, in the providence of God such writers *have* shaped the form of our literary landscape. If this is where we live, and it is, and this is our yard, we might as well settle in and mow the grass. Our students should study an interrelated body of literature.

And as they learn to do so, they will grow into themselves, self-conscious heirs of our culture in literature. "But in reading great literature I become a thousand men and yet remain myself. Like the night sky in the Greek poem, I see with a myriad eyes, but it is still I who see. Here, as in worship, in love, in moral action, and in knowing, I transcend myself; and am never more myself than when I do."[11]

---

[11] C.S. Lewis, *An Experiment in Criticism* (London: Cambridge University Press, 1969), p. 141.

FOURTEEN:

The Why and How of Rhetoric
Douglas Wilson

Rhetoric is the art of speaking clearly and *effectively*. Or, as Aristotle would put it, rhetoric is understanding and using the available means of persuasion. Of course, before a man can speak clearly and effectively, he must be able to *think* clearly and effectively. If *he* does not know what he is saying, it is unlikely that anyone else will. As Cato stated, "Grasp the subject, the words will follow."[1] This is why a mastery of the grammar and dialectic of education must precede the teaching of rhetoric.

This should be great with everybody, right? Our modern statist educators are certainly big on teaching "critical thinking skills." The popular bumper sticker which enjoins us to "Question Authority" is a popular illustration of this kind of thinking. This is the mentality which questions, differs, probes, and disagrees, but it does so in a relativistic fashion. It thinks critically about the "proposed answer" because it doubts that there are any answers. In short, it doubts everything except the reliability of its own doubting. The only authority which is respected is that of self—down to the ground, it is a subjective approach.

---

[1] *"Rem tene, verba sequentur."* Stanley Bonner, *Education in Ancient Rome* (Berkeley, CA: University of California Press, 1977), p. 11.

A logical answer to the bumpersticker (for those of us who talk back to bumperstickers) should be, "Says who?" Why are we being told, with authority, to question authority? A logical questioner has been trained to recognize such self-refuting problems, correct them, and arrive at a right answer. But of course, the use of phrases like "right answer" exasperates proponents of teaching critical thinking skills. "Right answers" are seen as dictatorial, authoritarian, and rough on a student's self-esteem. This is quite right. For the fuzzy-thought brigade, logic is positively tyrannical. But God reigns with justice; those who will not submit to *His* authority wind up submitting to the authority of self-contradictory bumper stickers.

Those who seek to inculcate "critical thinking skills" presuppose the authority of the questioner. He examines, probes, questions, and so forth, before he settles upon "whatever works for him." This approach presupposes the primacy of questions, based on the subjective authority of the one with the questions. But logical analysis presupposes the *objective authority of argument.* This approach assumes the primacy of validly derived answers. The reasoner is not at all interested in whatever would work for him; he is interested in what would be the case if he had never been born. In other words, he is interested in objective truth, derived from a sound argumentation. Nevertheless, appearances can be deceiving. The sophistry of "critical thinking skills" does enable educators to make intelligent-sounding noises while wandering relativistically in a circle. Christian educators should not be fooled by it. It is nothing more than sophisticated and witty chatter on the edge of the void. Such chatter can in no way be considered as the rhetoric which needs to be taught in a classical and Christian school.

In an essay on rhetoric, this is said about logic first because, in a biblical context, speaking clearly and effectively cannot be separated from the foundation of thinking clearly and effectively. This point must be made and emphasized because unfortunately, in our modern world, the word *rhetoric* is associated with the opposite of clear thinking—it is either associated with muddled thinking or deceitful thinking. No easier way exists to dismiss an opponent's arguments than by saying his case is "just a bunch of rhetoric."[2] The problem illustrates why it is necessary to plead for straight thinking as an introduction to this subject. Rhetoric as a discipline has fallen into disrepute. Consequently, before we may insist that our students think clearly about whatever subject they intend to address, we must think clearly about this subject.

Rhetoric Schmetoric

In the popular understanding, rhetoric is overblown bombast, style without meaning. In this use of the word *rhetoric*, words are substituted in place of ideas by politicians, to keep them out of trouble. In short, the popular view is that rhetoric is just a bunch of nothing. This is one of our more notable examples of a word coming to mean the opposite of what it is supposed to mean. This popular definition of rhetoric (accompanied by a popular dislike for it) is probably well exemplified by the speaking and writing of the late Warren Harding. One observer said, "His speeches leave the impression of an army of pompous phrases moving over the landscape in search of an idea. Sometimes these meandering words would actually capture a straggling thought and bear it triumphantly a prisoner in their midst until it died of servitude and overwork." H.L. Mencken was less kind. "He writes the worst English that I have ever encountered. It reminds me of a string of wet sponges; it reminds me of tattered washing on the line; it reminds me of stale bean soup, of college yells, of dogs

---

[2] "I do not think (and no great civilization has ever thought) that the art of the rhetorician is necessarily vile. It is in itself noble, though of course, like most arts, it can be wickedly used." C. S. Lewis, *A Preface to Paradise Lost* (London: Oxford University Press, 1942), p. 53.

barking idiotically through endless nights. It is so bad that a sort of grandeur creeps into it . . ."[3] This sort of bloviating fustian, at which Harding apparently excelled, is offensive to all, and almost all think that it is a good example of "rhetoric." It is not.

We may define a *rhetor* as one "skilled in speaking who addresses a public audience in order to make an impact upon it."[4] The language of such public speaking is commonly loftier than ordinary discourse, but when it is effectively done it does not draw attention to itself. This is because the one speaking is skilled at what he is doing, and churning up the hostility of an audience is not evidence of any skill. The point is to move the audience, but not towards the door.

The audience must be considered. Someone who has been taught rhetoric is not a windup doll, which goes out and speaks without taking into account the tastes and assumptions of the audience. Consequently, rhetoric, when it is done right, is largely invisible to the audience in front of the speaker. The Victorians had a taste for more flowery language than we do, so a rhetor speaking to an audience of Victorians could properly be more flowery than we would like to hear. If we were reading such a speech, we would notice as glaring problems certain things which would not be noticed at all by the original audience. These embellishments are not essential to rhetoric; they are essential when addressing certain kinds of audiences.

Rhetoric is designed for a more formal occasion. A man may think clearly, and talk to himself. He may chat with friends, sitting around the living room. Despite his clear thinking, and despite his use of speech, we would not think of saying that he is using rhetoric. Rhetoric proper is to be used in a formal setting—originally in the courtroom or forum.

---

[3] Quoted in Nancy McPhee, *The Book of Insults* (New York, NY: Penguin, 1978), pp. 124-125.

[4] Peter Dixon, *Rhetoric* (New York, NY: Methuen, Inc., 1971), p. 2.

Rhetoric is also an important point of integration in the classical curriculum. This essay began by emphasizing the importance of logical analysis. Logical precision is absolutely essential to rhetoric, and the study of formal logic elsewhere (and earlier) in the curriculum is a great asset in rhetoric, and essential to it. Likewise, the study of poetry and great literature in the various literature courses of your school has a close connection to rhetoric. Poetry and good writing expose the student to manners of expression and figures of speech which will be a great benefit to that student in rhetoric. Apologetics and rhetoric are also close sisters. Just as apologetics ties all the various subjects together in the light of the biblical worldview, so rhetoric enables the student to do so winsomely.

Character is also important. In spite of the opposition of many who say that rhetoric is essentially dishonest (starting with the opposition of Socrates), the traditional position taken by rhetoricians is that a rhetor must be a good man. In the classical understanding of rhetoric, the character of the speaker is important; many issues are tied together in the practice of rhetoric, including the character of the speaker. No evil man can be a rhetorician, but is rather a demagogue.

Moreover, he must have a natural aptitude for the calling. "The good orator must be a born orator, with a natural genius for his art. He will attain mastery by the study of theory, by assiduous practice in the courtroom or forum, and through the habit of imitation."[5] No school, no instructor of rhetoric, can put in what God left out. At the same time, even a "natural" who believes that this sort of thing can be done effortlessly will simply squander the talents God has given him.

An Outline of Classical Rhetoric

If the reader has followed the argument outlined above, then it should be clear that there is no "one size fits all" approach

---

[5] Dixon, *Rhetoric*, p. 23.

to rhetoric. The rhetor cannot develop a set stump speech and hit the road with it, expecting that anyone in the world would want to hear it, just as it is. Understanding this is part of rhetorical skill. Neither should rhetoric be associated with the sort of speaking skills which can be gathered from Toastmasters, or an average speech class. The positive skills to be learned there are certainly a part of rhetoric (*e.g.* "Don't mumble."), but the idea of rhetoric goes far beyond this simple or plain approach. Cicero distinguished three different types of oratory. The first was *genus grande* —the grand style. Here the speech was composed of great and impressive words, and arranged with a good deal of ornament. This may make many moderns squeamish, making them think of Harding's wet sponges, but it should really make us think of Churchill speaking to England at war. He had nothing to offer them but "blood, sweat, and tears"—and his rhetoric moved them the way rhetoric should. This high style is designed to move men.

The second style is the middle style which is considerably less elevated. It is more relaxed, but would never degenerate into slang. The purpose of this second, or middle, style is to please or entertain an audience.

The last can be called the simple or plain style (*genus humile*). This last style uses a conversational manner, and will include idioms from contemporary speech. The purpose of this style is to instruct an audience, or prove a point. Of course, the trained student of rhetoric will select the correct manner of address best suited for the occasion.

The "life" of the speech is distinguished in the following ways. The first is *inventio*, or invention. The speaker must first determine what he is going to say. The second element is *dispositio*, or arrangement. How will the various things to be said be arranged or ordered? The third is *elocutio* or style. How will it be said? Particular emphasis should be placed here on the three distinctions of style mentioned above. The fourth element is memory—the process of committing to memory what one is going to say. The last element is delivery. The various rules and divisions of classical rhetoric are arranged under these heads.

The *structure* of the speech can be arranged as follows:

The first thing to be presented to the audience is the *exordium* or introduction. The hearers need to get used to the sound of the speaker's voice before he tries to get them to think about anything. The idea is not to sway the listener but to get him into the right frame of mind. And, because classical rhetoricians loved to divide and subdivide again, they went on to distinguish two types of openings—the *direct* and the *indirect*. The indirect would be used, for example, if the crowd were a hostile one and resistance needed to be overcome.

The second portion of the talk would be the short *narratio*, which is a brief statement of the facts of the case. "This is what we are talking about."

Then the rhetor will put before his hearers the *propositio*. Here he sets the concern of the speech before his audience. Connected to this is the *divisio*, where the speaker presents a breakdown of the subject under certain main heads. A speech with seventeen main points would only muddle the audience, and classical rhetoricians thought that the best number to use would be three. This is the ancestor of the famous and well-known "three point sermon outline."

Next comes *confirmatio*, where the various arguments in support of the case are presented. By the eighteenth century, it was recommended that the strongest arguments be presented last. Then, in case there are any boneheads in the audience who are still unconvinced, the next portion—*refutatio*—will attempt to disarm or answer any anticipated objections.

The conclusion, or *peroration*, obviously comes last. It consists of three main parts. First the speaker sums up what he has said—*enumeratio*. Then the speaker will reassert his position—*amplificatio*. He will then appeal to the feelings and sentiments of the audience (*commiseratio*).

Dixon notes that this structure is not the result of classical and medieval rhetoricians running amok with their passion for order. "This elaborate structural scheme was the outcome of much theorising and *much practical experience.*"[6] An analogy may be helpful here, at least perhaps to any readers who perceive this as too contrived or artificial. The outline or arrangement of a speech along these lines can be treated as a skeleton. If the skeleton is visible, the appearance will be thought grotesque. But if the skeleton is there, giving structure to the talk, yet invisible to the audience, the effect will certainly be *pleasure* on the part of the listener.

Many other aspects of the study of rhetoric have not been mentioned here. After all, students will be taking it as course which culminates their study of many other subjects, over a period of many years. The central purpose here has been to reject the idea that rhetoric is bombast, and to give a very short introduction to some elements of the subject. If the study of rhetoric were to be thought a speech, what I have mentioned here is simply the *exordium*—the first few steps on to the front porch.

---

[6] Dixon, *Rhetoric*, p. 30. Emphasis mine.

FIFTEEN:

The Why and How of Apologetics

Douglas Jones

Some of the most hard-hearted agnostics and atheists are those who have trudged through years of Christian education. Many attended decent Christian schools, which gave scant analysis of non-Christian thought. The students then trotted off excitedly into the swift, spinning blades of a non-Christian university. Once there, the subtleties and surface sophistication of the instructors make dad, mom, pastor, and Christian high school teacher sound like academic Eeyores. Of course, the primary responsibility for such rebellion has to lie ultimately with parents who—however painful it is to accept—failed over the years to reveal the beauty of Christ in day-to-day family life (Prov. 22:6; 29:17). Deep, genuine, and pervasive Christian living is the only convincing apologetic for those close to us.

Nonetheless, we may not omit training in *apologetics*—the defense of our Christian hope (1 Pet. 3:15; 2 Cor. 10:5). The Spirit uses such argumentation in drawing and molding a people for Himself. Many apologetics courses, however, are rather shortsighted. They try only to patch a few holes here and there. They parry only a handful of mundane thrusts. But that is not the image of the Christian mind we find in Scripture. Scripture calls us and our students to a full-fledged *Christian skepticism*. What is that?

Christian Skepticism

Both of these words are crucial. Let's start with the second. We most often use the term *skepticism* when speaking about non-Christian scoffers—atheists, agnostics, and other such afflictions. But this is terribly misleading and unjustified.[†] In this common usage, a skeptic is someone who on the basis of some criterion of evidence rejects supernatural claims of many sorts, including Christian teaching on creation, fall, redemption. They regularly deny the existence of the triune God, prophecy, Christ's virgin birth, resurrection, and perhaps even His existence.

But notice this: they are not skeptics about every claim to knowledge. They hold fast to some standards of knowledge (scientific, logical, practical, *etc.*) by means of which they reject these other supernatural claims. So they are not what has been termed *global* skeptics, that is, those who deny humans can know anything at all. Probably no such animals have ever existed. How could they? By far the predominant meaning of *skepticism* is that termed *local* skepticism, that is, a view which denies knowledge of particular subjects, such as morality and the supernatural, but not, say, of science, mathematics, and logic.

Given this understanding, we can see why it is misleading and unjustified to reserve *skepticism* for non-Christian scoffers of the supernatural. We should call anyone a skeptic who invokes "legitimate" standards to shower doubt on other claims to knowledge. Nothing in *skepticism* limits its use to non-Christian standards. In fact, those non-Christians who

---

[†] Consider this comment from Malcolm Muggeridge, speaking of Pascal. "Like all true believers, he was deeply skeptical. His intelligence was wonderfully astringent and critical. It is one of the fantasies of the twentieth century that believers are credulous people, sentimental people, and that you have to be a materialist and a scientist and a humanist to have a skeptical mind. But of course exactly the opposite is true." Malcolm Muggeridge, *The End of Christendom* (Grand Rapids, MI: Eerdmans, 1980), p. 4.

most commonly bear the banner of skepticism always bandy about criteria of science and logic of a highly questionable and mysterious nature, given *their* take on the world. They rarely reflect on the legitimacy of their own standards of knowledge, preferring to trust in them rather blindly. The beauty of local skepticism is that it does not allow ideas to go unchallenged so easily. It asks plenty of questions. Many times, it asks the simple yet devastating "emperor-has-no-clothes" sort of question.

Now when we join this notion of skepticism to a Christian outlook, the resulting *Christian skepticism* is refreshingly cogent. It means that we leave nothing unchallenged in non-Christian claims. Nothing deserves the benefit of the doubt. Everything is guilty until proven innocent. Unless non-Christians can provide some solid reason for their claims about logic, science, *etc.*, then we should deem non-Christian claims empty fictions, pure mythology, blind faith.

Christian skepticism suggests that we challenge and doubt whatever fails to live up to the ultimate standard of knowledge—the mind of the Christian God. If Christianity is true, this is the only rational course of action, since God Himself is the highest standard of truth available. He has no superior beyond Himself. He is the Supreme Court of rationality. Every other standard of knowledge such as common sense, logic, science, the Church, *etc.* are helpful and important authorities, but they are all subordinate servants to God and His revelation in Scripture. When non-Christian skeptics balk at our criterion of knowledge, we can legitimately balk at their ultimate criteria in equal manner and show that theirs are far more questionable and suspicious.

This whole discussion cannot truly make sense unless we understand the deep hostility, the deep philosophical antithesis, between Christian and non-Christian thought. We are not two neutral parties skipping along hand-in-hand trying sincerely to live and let live. Scripture teaches us over and over again that the non-Christian heart and mind are hostile to the things of God, seeking to suppress God's honor, twisting His truth in selfish ambition. Because of this hostility to truth, Christians have an added reason to be suspicious of non-Christian claims. We would be foolish to let the claims of rebels stand on their own.

So the Christian skeptic and the non-Christian skeptic hold to opposing ultimate standards of knowledge that function in much the same way in evaluating beliefs and evidence. And both are suspicious about any of the claims to knowledge in the other camp. But the Christian skeptic is much more radical in his skepticism than his non-Christian counterpart. As noted above, the non-Christian skeptic will rarely talk about the *deep* foundational issues in knowledge. When the Christian skeptic begins to press and poke deep down in any non-Christian system, claims start to fly apart very quickly. Not much holds it together, and the more honest non-Christian philosophers know this, so they steer away from asking those sorts of questions.

Now this *does not* mean that Christians can not learn anything from non-Christian thinkers. At this time in history, non-Christian thinkers are regularly superior to Christian thinkers in their analysis of many issues. A healthy Christian skepticism will not reject every non-Christian claim, but it will doubt it and challenge it to determine whether it stands up under biblical scrutiny. Those genuine insights which remain, by the common grace of God, can be very helpful in constructing a Christian understanding of the world.

Scripture itself provides the basis for this broader understanding of Christian skepticism. Scripture not only speaks about the deep hostility non-Christians have for the God of Scripture, but it exhorts us to have a skeptical attitude toward non-Christian claims of wisdom.

In the Old Covenant, the prophet Jeremiah taught us about skepticism of the "wise" who set themselves up against God: "Who is the wise man who may understand this? . . . Let not the wise man glory in his wisdom. Let not the mighty man glory in his might, nor let the rich man glory in his riches. But let him who glories glory in this, that he understands and knows Me" (Jer. 9:12,23,24).

Similarly we read in the New Covenant, Paul's very skeptical declaration, which begins with a citation from a prophecy of Isaiah: "'I will destroy the wisdom of the wise and bring to nothing the understanding of the prudent.' Where is the wise? Where is the scribe? Where is the disputer of this age? Has not God made foolish the wisdom of this world?" (1 Cor. 1:19,20). In the same skeptical mode, Paul speaks of "the weapons of our warfare are not carnal but mighty in God for pulling down strongholds, casting down arguments and every high thing that exalts itself against the knowledge of God, bringing every thought into captivity to the obedience of Christ" (2 Cor. 10:4-5).

The Apostle also warns us, "Beware lest anyone cheat you through philosophy and empty conceit, according to the tradition of men, according to the basic principles of the world, and not according to Christ. For in Him dwells all the fullness of the Godhead bodily" (Col. 2:8,9). Thus, the Apostle describes non-Christian thought as an empty conceit, devoted as it is to the basic principles of this world, a philosophy in which man is the measure. Non-Christian mythology stands in contrast to that philosophy that is in accord with the principles of Christ in whom dwells the mind of God, the ultimate standard of truth and justice.

In sum, being a Christian skeptic is nothing new. It is simply part of the ancient Christian faith. It knows the hostility and futility of non-Christian thought, and so it knows non-Christian faith and ultimate standards are a failure. Non-Christian faith ultimately destroys knowledge. It deserves the radical skepticism with which Christians view it. But in order to be effective Christian skeptics, we must be trained in apologetics, not in a piecemeal fashion, but in all the depths and riches of the Christian faith. There is no way around it.

The Road to Christian Skepticism

All the declarations of Christian skepticism are quite empty without hard work and careful listening. So how can Christian parents and teachers prepare themselves for teaching apologetics?

Solid grounding in apologetics requires basic training in four areas: theology, philosophy, apologetical theory, apologetical practice. Let's take each in turn.

Theology

In order to be properly skeptical, we need to understand God's mind as much as humanly possible. That is an unending task, but in another sense, Scripture itself tells us that we can have the "whole counsel" of God within our grasp. Through diligent study we can grow in our understanding of the character and attributes of the triune God. If we fail to understand the truth, then we will be ineffective in spotting the counterfeits. So often in the history of the Church, God's people failed to adequately understand the dichotomy between Christianity and non-Christianity. Instead of protecting their thinking from the pagan idols surrounding them, they tried to mix the two, not recognizing the inherent hostility between Jehovah God and the gods of Assyria, Babylon, Greece, and the "Enlightenment."

What better place to learn theology than from Christ's Church? To it has been given the keys of the kingdom, and it has worked faithfully to summarize Christian truth in creeds and catechisms. Before purchasing all the new books on theology, go to the Church. Meditate on the early ecumenical counsels and their more mature expansion in the Reformation. In the *Westminster Confession* and catechisms, along with the *Belgic Confession* and *Heidelberg Catechism*, for example, you will see Christ's Church diligently seeking to clarify the biblical message and remove the compromises with pagan Greek thought so prominent in Roman Catholicism and Eastern Orthodoxy.

But however you gain a grasp of basic theology—the trinity, incarnation, creation, fall, covenants, justification, sanctification, law, fruit of the Spirit, eschatology—you must do it in order to do apologetics well. You must know and love what you are defending before you can enter the fray.

Philosophy

Knowing philosophy, especially the general contours of the history of non-Christian thought, is also essential for a robust Christian skepticism. Common apologetics is largely a defensive posture, but Christian skepticism goes on the offense in seeking to undermine non-Christian philosophies. And so in order to go on the offense, we must know the other side very well. If possible, we should understand their view much better than they know it themselves. If we fail to understand the subtleties of the opposition, then we will not be able to undermine it effectively. We may find ourselves fighting some irrelevant battle, when we should have been focusing elsewhere.

Having a working knowledge of the history of philosophy not only enables us to undermine the thinking of the opponents of Christ, it also enables us to spot it more readily when apparently well-meaning folks within the Church start inviting it in through the back doors. So many of the problems the Church has faced through the centuries have been internal compromises with pagan thought of one sort or another. Apologetics has its first place, perhaps, in guarding the interiors.

Finally, studying philosophy and theology are so important in order to develop sound reasoning skills. Courses in logic are important, but that resource is only good if it is exercised. By traversing centuries of arguments in philosophy and theology, one can examine and wrestle with some of the best argumentation available. Countless books introducing the history of philosophy and world religions are available in any good library.

Apologetical Theory

Each of these subjects builds on those before it. One will not do well in studying sound apologetical theory if one lacks a background in theology and philosophy. Good apologetical theory teaches us several main things to look for in a non-Christian worldview, such as its ultimate criterion of truth and its perennial inner conflict.

Every worldview, religion, or philosophical system has ultimate and subordinate criteria of knowledge (even those who profess to undermine knowledge, such as the postmodernists). The ultimate criterion of knowledge is that which divides truth and falsity, knowledge and mere opinion. Christianity has God's mind as revealed in Scripture as its ultimate criterion, but we also have *subordinate* criteria of varying authority in common sense, sense perception, reason, scientific methodology, the Church, *etc.*, all of which are genuine epistemological authorities, though subordinate to the ultimacy of Scripture. Non-Christian worldviews may find their ultimate court of appeal in sense experience or reason or mystical intuition or whatever, and that will be the idol the apologist focuses on. That idolatrous criterion is what they put in the place of God. Armed with a good knowledge of the history of philosophy, one can use a host of arguments in the past and present to demonstrate the failure of that ultimate idol.

Part of the road to undermining this ultimate criterion involves identifying the perennial inner tension in any non-Christian worldview. Every non-Christian worldview and religion is at odds with itself over its own claims of knowledge. The Christian skeptic must have an eye for picking out this tension. One way of describing this tension is in terms of *objectivity* and *subjectivity*. These are two of the most important words the Christian skeptic must master.

As used here, both of these terms describe things in the world. When we say something is subjective we mean that *it depends for its existence on something in a person's mind*, like an emotion, dream, idea, hope, belief, taste, *etc.* All these things are subjective to us, and if a person leaves the room he takes his hopes and beliefs with him. Ideas, emotions, *etc.* depend upon that person for their continuation. They do not exist independently from that person. So, if someone makes the wild claim that a cactus is subjective, then he is claiming that the cactus is a creation of his mind, a figment of imagination or something. Likewise, if he says God is subjective, then he is claiming that God is just an idea, not something out there outside of himself.

In contrast, when we say something is objective we mean that *it does not depend for its existence on us.* Something that is objective exists quite apart from us, like tables, cars, planets, other people, soap, and so on. Most things in the world exist independently from any one person. Unlike subjective things, when a person leaves a room the objective things remain (unless carried!). The table stays, but my hopes leave with me. So, if someone says that a car or a computer or the number two is objective, they mean that such things exist even if there are no minds around propping them up.

This distinction becomes particularly important when we start speaking of reason and morality. If reason and morality are subjective things, dependent upon humans, then to each his own, and there are no universal rules for thought or conduct. If, on the other hand, reason and morality are objective standards, existing quite apart from humans, then knowledge is possible.

In some form or another, the non-Christian always wants the criteria of knowledge to be both objective and subjective at the same time. This, obviously, is problematic, and it reveals the self-defeating nature of non-Christian thought. Consider some examples. Sometimes, the scientist and critic of the supernatural insists on the objectivity and universality of logic, scientific standards, *etc.,* but he also insists that these are products of chaotic, evolutionary nature, thus nonobjective and relative to each person. Likewise, the postmodernist denies the universality of logic and morality and yet appeals to objective standards in defending democracy and despising the morality of Christianity. New Agers, too, may virulently (by some objective standard) condemn Christian morality for its divisiveness and then in the same breath deny any distinction between good and evil, since all truth is intuitive and subjective.

Why do they do this? Why does this pattern show up so consistently in non-Christian thought? The short answer is that this sort of tension arises whenever one sets oneself up as the ultimate criterion of knowledge in place of God. As such you aim to set the universal rules (objectivity), and yet the world is beyond your knowledge and control (subjectivity). This is the heart of rebellion: denial of God and taking His seat.

This is just a very brief taste of apologetical theory. It goes much deeper, and the problems get harder, but this is a start, a start that depends so intimately on a good grounding in theology and philosophy.

Apologetical Practice

Theory without practice is rather lame. You cannot hope to teach students about apologetics unless you have had some real life practice which interacts with non-Christian counterarguments. But this is not always easy to find. Several options avail themselves though.

One way to start is to read actual debates between Christians and non-Christians. Christian publishers across the nation regularly print such debates in book form. Hunt these down and read them. Similarly, through the various apologetical ministries working around the nation you can find audio taped debates. These abound even more than the books and are sometimes more helpful, since the interactions are often more lively.

Even more interesting at present are the apologetical opportunities available on the Internet. Especially for beginning apologists, you have access to countless forums, discussion groups, *etc.* where you can interact with nonbelievers in a careful, thoughtful manner. Some discussions are set up just for these sort of debates. Begin by reading others' public discussions and then later join in yourself. Remember good apologetics is not a game, and you serve as an ambassador for Christ, always called to answer in a gentle manner.

Finally, in learning and teaching apologetics make sure you have plenty of access to non-Christian periodicals, especially of the secular, free-thought variety. You can find these in good college libraries and increasingly over the Internet. Focus on some anti-Christian essay and very thoughtfully seek to show yourself how you could apply apologetical theory to it. Work through about fifty anti-Christian articles in this way, being fair to the argument but showing how it ultimately undermines itself. If you create written responses, perhaps you can enter them in some Internet discussion area for feedback from non-Christians.

I have found that a close reading and discussion of the leading anti-Christian arguments is a tremendous benefit for high school students. It not only forces one to look at genuine non-Christian criticisms instead of weakened Christian caricatures, but it gives you and the students greater confidence when you realize how weak and futile the other side really is. After years of this sort of analysis, you can really start to appreciate the scriptural declaration, "Where is the wise? Has not God made foolish the wisdom of this world?" In the end, apologetics done to the glory of Christian God enhances the worship of God beyond anything you could imagine. Truly, you will then be able to say with all your heart and mind and strength, "Whom have I in heaven but You? And there is none upon earth that I desire besides You. My flesh and my heart fail; But God is the strength of my heart and my portion forever" (Ps. 73:25,26).

Section Three:

Making It Work In
This Century

SIXTEEN:

Understanding Bylaws, Policies, and Guidelines
Douglas Wilson

"But I thought you didn't believe in the Horn, Trumpkin,"
said Caspian. "No more I do, your Majesty. But what's
that got to do with it? I might as well die on a wild goose
chase as die here. You are my King. I know the difference
between giving advice and taking orders. You've had my
advice, and it's the time for orders."[1]

For a number of historical and theological reasons, Americans have a distorted perception of how biblical authority
works. We received a large measure of this distorted view in
the process of our *education*. Consequently, identifying the
problem is a matter of great importance, so that we do not
pass the problem on to our children in the process of *their*
education. Christians must seek to understand the nature of
authority, and must understand this task to be a central aspect of recovering a truly biblical education.

Authority works two ways, and, unfortunately, many
who set out to recover "authority" only recover one half of
it—the half that lets them give orders to someone else. But it
may be taken as axiomatic that someone does not have a biblical view of authority if he takes any less delight in *receiving*
instructions than he does in giving them. Submission is re-

---

[1] C.S. Lewis, *Prince Caspian* (New York, NY: Macmillan, 1951),
p. 92.

quired of all Christians, and of course someone who does not know how to submit is someone who is not to be entrusted with leadership.

There are some additional subtleties, however, which bear directly on the task of education. Most Christian schools operate under plural leadership—usually under the authority of a school board. Now Jesus taught that no man can serve two masters. How can this be reconciled with plural leadership? The pattern of plural, corporate leadership is certainly biblical (it is *required* in the church, for example). So how is it possible for administrators, teachers, staff and students under this plural authority to keep from being pulled in different directions, and all by people equally "in charge"? Tragically, in many schools this pulling in different directions is a pulling *apart*.

In order to remain biblical, all forms of plural leadership must speak with a *single voice*. Several examples should serve to illustrate the principle. Suppose a school board is in the process of selecting a line of textbooks. Suppose further there have been vigorous and thorough debates in the board meetings about the value of this publisher versus the value of that one. The day comes, however, when the vote is taken, and the school board has made its decision. Now—the board member in the minority must not only submit to the decision (which he obviously has to do anyway), he must also *support* it.

This idea horrifies us. So in order to maintain our unbiblical approach to authority, we immediately rush to "worst case scenarios." "But," we argue, "suppose the textbooks in question are put out by *Satan & Sons*—'We make humanism palatable for Christian schools!'"?

The answer here of course is that this is a school board from which godly Christians must resign. There are times when submission to human authority does constitute disobedience to God. No human authority is absolute; no human authority legitimately commands unquestioning obedience.

But if it is impossible to submit to a school board, then it is impossible to stay on that school board. If it is legitimate to stay, then it is required to submit. We cannot take a middle ground and say that this is a *big* enough issue to allow us to be noisy and unsubmissive and *small* enough to allow us to remain.

Suppose further that you are now at the meeting where the new textbooks are being announced, the minority board member is chairing the meeting, and a parent in the back row objects. He lists seven compelling reasons why the other textbooks should have been selected. They are the same seven compelling reasons that the chairman himself presented last week in the board meeting. Now the chairman only has a biblical view of authority if he now stands publicly with the rest of the board. It was not the *majority's* decision; it was the *board's* decision. A majority vote is simply the device chosen by the entire board for the entire board to make a decision. Once the vote is taken, the entire board has decided whether or not the vote was unanimous. If being identified with such a decision is sin, then a godly board member must leave the board. If being identified with the decision is not sin, then that board member must swallow his pride—*all of it*—and say, "We thought we should choose these textbooks because . . ."

A second example of this type of authority can be seen in the family. Father and mother are both in authority over the children. Let us say one of the children has been disciplined by the father, and suppose the mother is not in full agreement with how the discipline was administered. Should this concern be expressed? Of course—in private. As far as the children are concerned, the parents should always present a united front. Because parents are a form of plural leadership over children, they must speak with a single voice. When they do not, children learn very quickly how to play one parent off the other. And in the same way, a group of parents in a school can learn very quickly how to play one board member off another.

It is only in this way—the way of true submission—that plural leadership can speak with a single voice. As we consider the implications of this, it is obvious we all have much to learn. The board of a classical Christian school must therefore understand authority from the beginning. As discussed above, for board members, knowledge of biblical authority is measured by how individual members of a plural authority themselves behave under authority. A plural authority does not have has many voices as it has individual members. All godly plural leadership must have a single voice. This means full submission after the vote, and clear separation from the board if submission is a moral impossibility.

Problems can come out in other ways as well. Some board members like to "think out loud." And the speculations of just one board member may carry far more weight, and do far more damage, than one might think. "I think we should dismiss the students at 3:30 instead of 3:00. Just an idea." Other problems can be caused by disagreements in public between board members. The problem is not the disagreement—that is necessary for a healthy board—but rather a public airing of those disagreements. Discussion and disagreement should be saved for the board meetings.

Debates between individual board members and the administrator should never happen. If there is a difference of opinion (and there will be), the administrator should always have the opportunity to express his convictions, in detail, to the board. The board should be free to question him, in order to determine what his convictions are, as well as to see the foundation for them. *Under no circumstances* should any one board member be permitted to debate the administrator. The administrator would be an extraordinary man indeed if he did not feel that this disagreement was coming from the entire board—after all, one board member is speaking to him this way, and the others are letting him. The administrator should be completely heard, and then the issue debated within the membership of the board. Such debates are healthy and necessary—it is the way a board *thinks*.

But after the thinking is done, action must be taken. The board, along with everyone else who is associated with the school, should have a clear understanding of *what constitutes board action*. Board action is not "anything that happens at a board meeting." Logos School defines board action this way— "The board will be considered as having formally acted when, in a duly-constituted meeting, a proposal is moved, seconded, discussed, passed with the appropriate margin of votes, entered in minutes, and duly-approved."[2] The bylaws go on to note that board discussion, consensus, debate, *etc.* do *not* constitute formal board action. If these criteria are not met, then *the board has not acted*. It should become clear below that the bylaws and all school policy are to be considered board action, but not all board action is in the category of bylaw or policy. For example, if the board votes to hire someone, that is board action, but it is not a bylaw or policy. Nevertheless, *anything* which is to be considered board action must be established in the minutes. If it is not there, then the board has not spoken with a single voice, and various opinions of individual board members are just that—individual opinions.

As a school is being established, the highest priority should be given to the approval of bylaws, policies, and guidelines respectively. If a school is already established, but without a clear and approved definition of these, then disaster awaits. Schools which are up and running without a "constitution" are probably managed on the basis of day-to-day decisions by an administrator or board, and the resultant inconsistency plagues the management of the school. Oftentimes, the school's "policy manual" is an overstuffed Talmudic notebook—a jumble of minutes, *ad hoc* decisions, *etc.*

In order to establish bylaws, policies, and guidelines properly, the board must know what they are, and what their respective levels of authority are. *Bylaws* govern the entire school community, board included. The *policy manual* gov-

---

[2] Logos School Bylaws, Article VIII, Section 8.

erns the "in-house" operations of the school, and is the primary source of board direction to the administration. *Guidelines* are drafted and implemented by the school's administrators as they give direction to teachers, students, *et al.*

The Bylaws

govern the entire operation—particularly the board. It is at this point that the board demonstrates whether it has a biblical view of authority, whether the board is willing to be itself in submission. If the school is a biblical operation, it will be governed by law, and not by men operating in their own individual capacity. Of course, a certain type of godly board member is necessary for the success of any school—but one of the first characteristics of an individual who can be trusted is the fact that he does not trust himself, and wants to submit the school to a constitution.

Bylaws should set and define such things as the name of the school, and the school's objectives and statement of faith. The composition of the board should be set, along with the way board members become board members. Qualifications for board membership should be clear. The board itself should have officers (chair, vice-chair, secretary, *etc.*) and they should be set by the bylaws. Clear, defined procedures should be set for the removal of any board member. The bylaws should grant the board authority to establish an executive committee in order to conduct certain specified types of business.

The bylaws will establish the way in which regular meetings of the board are held, as well as any special meetings. They will define matters such as the decorum of all meetings, the number necessary for a quorum, the procedures for meeting in executive session, and so forth. As mentioned earlier, what constitutes board action should be defined.

The bylaws should also define the areas of fiscal responsibility—budgets, financial statements, financial accountability, and fund-raising. The same extends to the area of contracts, loans, checks and drafts, and deposits. The bylaws should define the fiscal year for the school.

Lastly, they should define the procedure for amendments to the bylaws. Because the board is *under* the authority of the bylaws, the board should not have the authority to amend the bylaws without public notification of the school's constituency of the nature of the change, and the reasons for it. No change should be permitted unless full opportunity for a response from the school's constituency has been given. In other words, the board is the entity which has the authority to amend the bylaws, but because the board is accountable to those bylaws, this should never be done "in secret." The purpose is public accountability, and that purpose must not in any way be circumvented.

Policies

Policies are determined by the board. They regulate board action and are also the principal means of giving direction to the administration.

A common mistake which committed boards often make is that of micro-management. Board members are often visionaries who care very much how the school is managed and governed. This is as it ought to be. But unless everyone concerned watches these distinctions carefully, the board will find itself considering the *Toilet Paper Roll Rotation Policy 6.2.*

Policy should therefore be, in a certain way, detached and distant from the day-to-day operations of the school. If the board is too close, it will resort to ongoing crisis management, and will perpetually annoy their administrator, who was hired to do what the board is trying to do. The board is not supposed to be "on the spot." A good board is distant, objective, Olympian, aloof. The board should be passionately committed to the vision of the school, but the board's job is to *articulate* that vision, and then *delegate*. The board must not try to be the executive which implements that vision. A board which tries to muscle in on the administrator's tasks *cannot* be a good administrator, and apparently *will not* be a good board.

When the board wants to see a change in how the school is run, the board should pass a policy which addresses the situation in question, *and all other situations like it*. Another way of putting this is that in dealing with policy the board should be concerned with *genus* and not with *species*. If a student shows up with tuberculosis, the response should not be a tuberculosis policy, but rather the problem should have been anticipated with a communicable disease policy. Such policies mean that the administrator knows what to do when any particular situation arises.

Individual cases should come before the board rarely, and that as a result of the administration's application of policy. For example, say that the board has a policy on academic dismissal from the school—*i.e.*, a student must be dropped from the program if his grade point drops below a certain level for two consecutive quarters. Because this is the policy, the administrator has his instructions and will drop a student if that happens. Now, suppose the parents want to appeal this decision. The appeal would have to be made to the board, but, importantly, it would only come to the board by means of *appeal*. The board is not involved because they knew about the situation from the beginning.

A good policy manual will reiterate some of the boundaries set by the bylaws, and go on to provide a structure within which the school operates. The policy manual should acknowledge both the school's statement of faith, and go on to state the educational philosophy of the school, referring by name to certain books and articles which capture what the school is trying to do. This means that administrators are authorized and required to use these materials designated in the school's policy manual as a basis of training for the staff. For two examples, the policy manual for Logos School mentions both Dorothy Sayers' essay *The Lost Tools of Learning*, and John Milton Gregory's *The Seven Laws of Teaching*. The school's commitment to the principle of *in loco parentis* should also be acknowledged here, as well as the way the school will handle divisive doctrinal issues.

Echoing the bylaws, but with a little more specificity, the policy manual should define the organization and operation of the board, the board's major responsibilities (*e.g.*, approval of the annual budget), the board calendar, recognition of board committees, and the procedures used by the board in making policy. The policy manual should define the school's administrative personnel—superintendent, principals, development officer, office staff, *etc*.

The board should set policies for school operations and equipment, ranging from facility maintenance to the care and feeding of any bus the school owns which might be still running. The policy manual should define how the board determines compensation and benefits, biblical guidelines for fundraising, procedures for paying bills (including overdue bills), fee collection, capital expenditures, and so forth.

The board should have personnel policies (hiring, assignments, retention, certification, evaluations, firing, grievances, etc.). The policy manual should also have a section which addresses the academic program of the school (curriculum, academic probation, extracurricular activities, discipline procedures).

In all these policies, it must be remembered that the board is not addressing any particular situation, but rather a particular situation and any other like it. While a particular "story" lies behind many policies, a well-written policy speaks broadly and not just to one narrow situation.

Guidelines

Guidelines are to be determined by the administration. When the board has taken action (whether in the bylaws, in the policy manual, or in a minuted individual action), the task of the administrator is to see that this decision is implemented. To return to an earlier example, that of academic dismissal from the school: say that the board has determined that a student is to be dismissed if his grades fall below a certain level for two consecutive quarters. The superintendent, in applying this decision, may give certain guidelines to his staff on how to deal with a student, and his family, if he is in danger of dismissal (timely communications, *etc.*). These guidelines are consistent with the policy, and are a means of implementing it, but have a greater specificity than the policy itself.

Conclusion

At every level of authority in the school—board, administration, staff—there should be a good understanding of the differences between bylaws, policies, and guidelines. Bylaws have the highest authority, policy has the next level of authority, and guidelines are next. Each is to be consistent with the level above. Moreover, as authority decreases, detail increases. However, the increasing detail must never be used to circumvent the higher authority.

SEVENTEEN:

Planning and Overseeing the Curriculum
Tom Garfield

Assumptions

In attacking a huge topic such as this one, a number of assumptions need to be made. The first assumption is that, as with almost anything worth doing, once you delve into the material, you quickly discover that there is always more information that can be discovered and applied. So this brief article unapologetically will take the tried-and-true "This is a football" approach; that is, it will stick to just basics. It is the author's hope that these basics will fit, for the most part, your particular situation, or at least satisfy your reason for reading this.

The second assumption here is that the reader avows all the primary tenets of Christianity; most importantly the view that the Bible is authoritative in everything that it addresses and that it addresses everything. Christian school curriculum falls under admittedly general category of "everything," so the assumption applies here.

The third and (for now) final assumption is that the reader (and any other person associated with a school) is willing to *work* and *think*. Curriculum development of any sort, but particularly in a Christian context, offers loads of potentially tedious and unavoidably time-consuming physical and mental wear-and-tear. "Potentially" is used here because, just like people who grow up to become accountants or census-takers, there are adults who actually enjoy working with the varied aspects of curriculum growth. However, love it or not, curriculum development is not an option of any serious Christian school. It must be done, and it must be done well. That means tons of work, which includes the willingness to never assume the task is ever totally done.

Definitions

Curriculum: To many people outside educational circles, *curriculum* is another word for policies or, almost as exciting, 'guidelines'. Even those individuals within or profoundly interested in education often misuse the term. One of the most frequent questions asked by prospective parents and others inquiring about Logos is "What kind of curriculum do you use?" Upon further questioning, it becomes apparent that what they are really asking is, "From what publisher(s) do you buy your texts?"

Let's set the record straight. *Curriculum*, as defined by the most authoritative sources, is *not* the materials a school uses, but rather "all the courses of study offered by an educational institution." The word curriculum itself comes from the Latin word *currere*, that is *to run*. Our word refers to a *course*, like a horse race track. So, to be accurate, a school's curriculum is actually made up of the entire course, or planned track, laid out for the students to complete.

Goals: As Logos School uses the term *goals*, it means unreachable, idealistic (that is, reflective of the school's philosophy), but unique and worthy targets. For example: "Encourage every student to develop a love for learning and live up to his academic potential." How does one measure the success or attainment of such a statement? Will there ever come a time when the Logos School leadership can truly say—"100% of our students have attained this goal!"? Obviously not, unless we have a real problem with arrogance. Goals are nevertheless extremely necessary to provide the direction the curriculum needs.

Objectives: Course objectives, as opposed to goals, are by definition measurable. They should be precise statements of purpose, derived from the school's written, overall goals and philosophy, and applied to each separate grade/subject by level. These objectives then become the measures by which that portion of the program's overall progress is evaluated. For example: "By the end of the first grade reading program, the student will have successfully completed steps 1-24 in the Sing, Spell, Read, and Write phonics training." That is a quantifiable, objective measure, that a teacher can confidently use to determine how many and which students have mastered that portion of the reading program.

Scope and Sequence: When the school's goals, philosophy, and course objectives are pulled into one neat package, that construct is usually called the school's "Curriculum Guide", or its Scope and Sequence. In either case it becomes the written, overall "blueprint" for the teachers and administration to follow, since it describes the precise step-by-step progression of instructional program for the students in each distinct grade/subject. Obviously the parents should also be, and often are, interested in this document. Its practical use, however, lies in the clarity and consistency it offers to the school's staff. Class content, for instance, should not be largely left to the whims of the individual teacher. A document will usually last longer than a teacher, no matter how good that teacher may be. More will be said about the implementation and revision of the Curriculum Guide later.

Planning the Curriculum

The sound curriculum will be the relevant curriculum, and relevancy requires two factors, *a world of absolutes*, and a *world of change*. It is not enough to hold to God's absolutes: they must be continually and freshly related (*i.e.* applied) to the changing times.

R.J. Rushdoony

Is not the great defect of our education today . . . that although we succeed (?) in teaching our pupils "subjects", we fail lamentably on the whole in teaching them how to think: they learn everything, except the art of learning.

Dorothy L. Sayers

In planning a Christian school curriculum, don't start with material selection. Start with questions. Such as:

Know *what* it is your school hopes to achieve:

1. Ask yourselves (or the school) *lots* of questions . . . What will characterize a graduate from our school? How will we equip him to face the onslaught of the world? Will he have the tools to refute and answer intelligently those who confront him? What will be the measure by which we determine our success or failure? What biblical *principles* will shape our program? (Note: The Bible was never intended by God to be treated specifically as a math, science or history text. See assumption #2 above.)

2. Determine (or adapt from a successful school) the school's own unique Goals, Principles, Objectives, Curriculum Guide.

3. Do not solely rely on any (Christian or secular) publisher's knowledge/philosophy.

4. Be prepared with *biblical* (not reactionary) answers to the curriculum "faddishness" urged by our godless society, *e.g.,* What about sex/drug education? Environmental issues? Political correctness? Remember: "the best defense is a good offense!" Know the Word.

Elements to Include in Your Curriculum

1. Flexibility: Allow for the fact that though ageless absolutes and timeless skills are the foundational philosophy of a good curriculum, the world has a changing face (as mentioned above). Some ways to help evaluate those changes are:

a. Don't "marry" materials or publishers; rather commit to a God-centered *vision*. This articulated vision will enable a school to sort through all the new offerings and possibly find some useful tools. Go ahead and plunder the Egyptians! See below for more on selecting materials.

b. Incorporate plans for regular evaluation, revision, and teacher-input. At Logos, our school board assigned our Curriculum Committee the task of reviewing all the major disciplines in a five-year cycle. For example, in one year the topic might be Science. In that year, then, the committee breaks into elementary and secondary subcommittees and examines every aspect of the science curriculum. When we did this several years ago, after many hours of work applying our particular purposes and philosophies to the respective levels, we came up with a science program that was uniquely ours from bottom to top.

c. Allow for a variety of students; they are not identical in learning styles or abilities. Set high standards within the objectives, but allow the teachers some flexibility for varying rates of progress, especially in reading and math. Borrowing materials from grades above and below is a practical means of helping a wide range of students.

2. Functional Format: Making the Curriculum Guide as clear as possible in its format and presentation is critical if the teachers are to use it on a regular basis. This is especially important for the uncertain and uneducated (normally in classical methodology) new teachers. How many well-thought out, but overweight, impractical guides sit on classroom shelves, or gather dust even in administrators' offices? Some ideas for making it a really useful tome:

a. Use a consistent format (structure) for each grade and separate class. For instance, each class's guide, from kindergarten through twelfth grade, should include at least: a list of materials used for that subject; the list of objectives for the year ("The student will be able to . . ."); the best means/

methods of teaching the subject (including the recommended classical methods); and some idea of how long the class is per day.

b. Keep it as concise and practical as possible; the guide is where philosophy is applied, not where it should be thoroughly discussed. A brief summary of each department's unique Christian and classical approach may be a part of the curriculum guide for the secondary, but it is used primarily for training for the teachers.

c. Administrators should build in ways of incorporating the use of the guide, such as making the reading of the guide part of the orientation of the teachers. Later in the year, require its use for the teachers' construction of quarterly or semester goals. Finally, the guide (and its objectives) should be part of the evaluation(s) completed on each teacher's progress.

d. Review the format with the teachers frequently (annually) to see if they think it could be better presented.

Selecting Curriculum Materials

1. First big question: Will the school use teacher-taught materials or individual-pace materials (such as the A.C.E.— Accelerated Christian Education—program)? Obviously, there are pros and cons to both. If there is a real diversity of opinion on this issue, first of all compare the benefits/problems of both to the school goals. Contact schools using both and get their assessments. However, be sure to also get a copy of their school philosophies and goals.

2. Second big question: Will the school use Christian publishers only, or mix of secular and Christian? A vital reminder: *never settle for low quality just because it's a "Christian" brand name publisher.* Not only is that dishonoring to the work of the Lord; it will be a detriment to the students. When Logos first began, we adopted virtually all the materials we used in the school from a single, popular Christian publisher. Because of our preset philosophy on education and God's Word,

we quickly became disenchanted with this publisher. Why? Simply because it taught, in addition to the basic content, that out-of-context Bible passages could be shoehorned into just about any subject. It also discouraged the application of biblical principles in approaching a subject, and instead, relied on stating didactic opinions as truth. This served to force us to reexamine why we taught what we taught in our overall course for Logos. It forced us to develop our own curriculum guide and objectives, in addition to our philosophy and goals.

Unfortunately, many Christian and home schools blithely assume that "if it's a Christian publisher, it must be okay." In addition to the publisher's world view, overall quality of the text is often overlooked or excused on the basis of the text's "Christian" status. Generally speaking, Christian publishers are often behind the times in terms of presentation quality and even content accuracy, such as up-to-date scientific discoveries (not theory, facts). However, those same publishers are on a sharp learning curve, so they are well-worth seeking out first, with certain guidelines in place. At the end of this chapter, see the Logos School policy on selecting textbooks and materials.

The secular materials have obvious philosophical problems, but also, they are even including actual mistakes, at an alarmingly increasing rate. Case in point: the wave of concern a few years ago brought about by gross errors being found in many widely used secular U.S. History texts. The final tally, as reported in an article in the *Wall Street Journal*, was about 5,200 mistakes! They included errors like FDR dying in 1944 instead of 1945; Napoleon winning at Waterloo, or Truman using an A-bomb on Korea in the 50's.

Christian parents who have their children in a government school and, because their children appear to be doing well morally and academically, never closely examine that school's curriculum, are like the followers of Crazy Horse. Because of Crazy Horse's teaching in the late eighteen hundreds, a number of Indians believed that if they did a special dance the white men's bullets wouldn't harm them, and, even more, that the white men would leave. The wounds these students are receiving are mental and spiritual; the wounds may not bleed, but they will just as effectively cripple and maim the student's thinking for years to come. News flash: Secular curricula today not only disregard accuracy in history, they actively ignore the biblical tradition of our country, they frequently promote homosexuality as an acceptable lifestyle, they often have a pro-abortion stance, and they belittle a traditional family structure. They do all this and more, without any warning labels on the covers! For a more thorough examination of history-teaching trends, contact Wallbuilders, Inc., in Texas.

3. Remember, *everybody*, including Christian publishers, wants to sell their products. Examine each separate product; do not ever buy *en masse*.

4. Big is not always better; seek out, smaller specialty publishers (Greenleaf Publications, Institute for Creation Research, Moody Press, or God's World [examples in the Christian realm], Social Studies School Service, Educators' Publishing Service, Saxon Math [examples in the secular realm]).

5. Ask others (schools, teachers) what *they* use and why. Ask A.C.S.I. (Association of Christian Schools, International) for textbook surveys (most recently done in 1995). This may save a lot of time and footwork in finding possible titles to choose from, but it won't remove the need for each school to evaluate each title being considered.

6. Establish selection and ordering procedures that are followed each time. Use current and senior teachers on the curriculum and selection committees, along with the pertinent administrators. Parents with applicable expertise can be inestimably valuable, as long as they know what is expected of them. A lot of money can be saved and frustration avoided by being critical of a text, versus an attitude of wanting to favor it, for whatever reason.

For smaller purchases, such as teacher resources, just providing the funds and support for the teacher can produce a very high quality teaching situation for the students. For example, Logos School's annual auction is partially designated for teacher discretionary spending. The teachers have a great time purchasing quality materials they otherwise wouldn't have bothered the administrator (and the budget) about.

7. Don't let the administrator be a Scrooge; if the materials/texts will significantly aid the teachers' in completing the set objectives and is of high quality, plan to purchase them. Perhaps the teachers' making their own materials (including publishing their own texts) may come with experience. Don't expect teachers to do this before their third year.

8. Look for bargains, free exam copies; tell the publishers that the school is considering placing an order. Ask about pilot programs and never say *no* to offers of donated materials; even if it's junk now, next time the offer from that same person may include some gems.

Conclusion

It matters what curriculum the school follows. It is the blueprint, albeit somewhat subject to added improvements, upon which the "house"—the school's reputation and mission- will be built. As Charles Spurgeon put it, "Have a care what you are after; you are teaching children; mind what you are doing. Put poison in the spring, and it will impregnate the whole stream. Take care what you are after, sir! You are twisting the sapling, and the old oak will be bent thereby." Plan well and the "oaks" will be straight and tall, and with prayer, may be planted by "streams of living waters."

Chapter Appendix:
Logos School Curriculum Materials Selection Policy

Objective: To help ensure that the philosophical and scriptural goals of Logos School are being adequately reinforced through the curriculum materials selected for each core class.

Scope: This policy applies to all nonelective (core) courses taught in the elementary and secondary levels of Logos School.

Definitions: "Core courses"—Those subject areas normally considered indispensable to an adequate education: Bible, math, science, history, English, literature, foreign languages.

Guidelines: Selection of materials

No curriculum materials with a secular worldview may be adopted for student use unless all the following conditions have been considered:

1. After thorough research there appear to be no biblically-based materials of equal or better quality to the secular materials.

2. The secular material's primary document status necessitates it be used to fulfill adopted course objectives.

3. After a thorough examination, it is determined that while secular in intent, the materials do not undermine, but rather support broad biblical truths (*e.g.* a high quality, secular mathematics text, or high quality, timeless literature).

Guidelines: Adoption of materials (Elementary)

All core materials for elementary student use may only be adopted through the following procedures:

1. A teacher or administrator may make the recommendation to add or delete a student text. This may be done at any time, but is normally submitted at the end of the school year during the annual evaluation period.

2. In most cases, unless it would significantly alter the purposes and objectives of the coursework, the decision for replacement of a text/materials will be left to the appropriate administrator, teacher(s), any advisory individuals and budgetary considerations.

3. All such substitutions of texts/materials must comply with the above considerations for using secular materials.

4. Should a member of the school (parent, teacher, board member, administrator) wish to challenge the adoption/use of a particular text/material, or if the proposed selections would conflict (rather than support the previously adopted course objectives) the matter will be referred to the curriculum committee for recommended action. Should this not result in a satisfactory solution, the matter will be referred to the school board.

Guidelines: Adoption of materials (Secondary)
All core materials for secondary student use may only be adopted through the following procedures:

1. A teacher or administrator may make the recommendation to add or delete a student text. This may be done at any time, but is normally submitted at the end of the school year during the annual evaluation period.

2. Requests for additions or deletions of materials for student use will be submitted through the secondary principal to the curriculum committee.

3. All such substitutions of texts/materials must comply with the above considerations for using secular materials.

4. The future availability, as well as the durability, of the proposed text/materials will be considered by the curriculum committee.

5. Should a member of the school (parent, teacher, board member, administrator) wish to challenge the adoption/use of a particular text/materials; or if the proposed selections would conflict with (rather than support) the previously

adopted course objectives, the matter will be referred to the Curriculum Committee for recommended action. Should this not result in a satisfactory solution, the matter will be referred to the school board.

Guidelines: Use of secular materials (at any level)
When secular materials have been adopted for student use, the following guidelines must be adhered to:

1. The secular material must be rigorously examined and countered in philosophy with biblical/true perspectives (*e.g.* presenting the elements of the Theory of Evolution is desirable, but it must subjugated in time and emphasis to the elements of the Creation account), in keeping with the scope of the course.

2. Falsehoods and unbiblical philosophies must be always identified as such.

3. Biblical principles within and/or related to the course objectives must also be presented to the students (*e.g.* while using a secular United States history text, the teacher must identify and emphasize the biblical foundations of our country).

EIGHTEEN:

The Servant School
Tom Garfield

The Classical School and the Family

"Don't mess with me, I'm a professional!" One of the greatest mistakes made by many Christian schools, classical or otherwise, is not having a very good understanding of what our role is as Christian educators, in relation to the governments God has established. Certainly I am pleased and even proud to be a professional Christian school administrator and teacher because of the work I am privileged to do each day in the lives of these students. But there is a form of "professionalism" that goes beyond the bounds God has laid.

In the teaching profession currently, we have, speaking broadly, lost the sense of a servant mindset. The government or public school mentality, though only about one hundred and fifty years old, has radically altered the way we all, Christian or pagan, look at school teachers.

This is not the place to go into a exhaustive treatise on the history of education. Nevertheless, only a little over a hundred years ago in this country, teachers in the forming frontier towns, especially out west here, were given a lot of respect, if not much money. That respect was shown because of the work they did with the children. But their role was seen as a servant to the parents. Families understood and everyone took for granted that fact that getting kids "schooled" was a familial responsibility. After the church was built, which was usually the first thing done in a town, the schoolhouse was erected and the teacher was hired. The teacher would often live with, and spend much time in the homes of, the town's families. Since the room and board were provided, pay was extremely low for teachers. The teacher would usually be a single young man, sometimes a young woman (very rarely a married woman), and living with the families of the school children was done as a matter of course. This also indicated the high regard in which the teachers were held by the parents. Strict rules of proper behavior, laughed at today, were serious conduct codes for teachers then. Teachers were actually expected to be role models to the children, even when not in school. In a small community that was very often the way it was: poor job conditions, but lots of respect.

Now, I'm not advocating that we return to those living arrangements. For example, I don't know anyone who would be able to take in my wife, my four children and me. However, I would advocate that we re-earn the role and respect our forerunners had. It is a very common, taken-for-granted attitude that we're all "professionals" of some kind. I find it very interesting that "professionals" of any ilk need to form unions and strike just as the factory workers did back in the 20's and 30's—closing down businesses, or in this case, schools, to get their demands met. Basically, strikes are a means of brute force to get the desires that the teachers are unable to achieve with more civilized means. That kind of strong-arm tactic just by itself changes peoples' perceptions of the teaching "profession." A strike is ugly, no matter who's doing it or for what reason. Doctors and lawyers are not often out in the street carrying signs for higher pay or other contract negotiations, but yet sign-carrying teachers yelling on the streets still want to be regarded as professionals. We've lost the sense of what that word means.

I've never had my children in the government schools, but I've been there myself, both as a student and a teacher. My parents had four children; we all grew up and went through the public school system in Michigan. My parents saw the teachers' attitudes change from that of servants to that of "professionals," and, like thousands of other parents, my folks felt powerless to address the change. Fortunately, my parents' primary teaching resource were still the Lord and His Word, so we children made it through without too many ill effects.

Sad to say, this "I'm a professional" attitude has carried over into the Christian realm. In a sense it was inevitable. Consider, where do we get our teachers? By and large we get them from the secular colleges of education. Young men and women who are interested in teaching—Christian or not—go through pretty much the same academic and certification hoops. They are taught from a specific, most likely worldly, philosophy. Unless the young person is unusually biblically astute, he will swallow the good with the bad: "You should be considered an autonomous professional once you get into the work place." "Don't let the parents or even the school board hamper your academic freedom." "Get your contract established with all the benefits you want right up front." "Children are basically good—they should be able to choose their own educational needs and lifestyle." On and on it goes. So it comes across, right down the line from the colleges, often unchecked, right into our schools (even our Christian and classical schools), if we are not ready to counter it with a planned program of biblical in-service teacher training.

Considering the Christian Home

Extremely few colleges, even Christian ones, teach teachers-to-be what the biblical role of the family is in education. A brief reminder here may be helpful, but your school will need a very clear and thorough way of communicating the school's commitment to the biblical family. All policies, guidelines, and even teaching methods should instruct the teachers about the school's view of the family.

In Genesis, after Adam and Eve were created, God established the family as the first human institution, with Adam clearly the leader (Genesis 2:23). The family was the institution created to have godly children, to multiply (have lots of kids), and to dominate (wisely use, not fearfully "save") the earth. These are very significant goals, all requiring extensive knowledge and training. From Deuteronomy, Proverbs, Ephesians, and other scriptural references, we understand that training children up in the Lord is a 24-hour-a-day, seven-day-a-week job. It is also clear from Scripture that the father, not the mother (even though she has the stronger nurturing impulse), has the responsibility to ensure his children are thoroughly trained, *i.e.*, educated well, in the Lord.

Well, golly, we as Christian educators know all that stuff, don't we? Yes, the above statements can and should be considered 'Christian Ed. 101.' The problem is that if we all know it so well, why don't our schools reflect it? Why are parents allowed to abdicate the responsibility for biblically educating their children in so many Christian schools? That's quite a charge. Allow me to elucidate. There are a variety of ways Christian schools allow this abdication to happen, or even encourage it. Let's look at the biggest, and possibly, most controversial area first: salvation.

How natural it is, or should be, for Christian parents to train their children up and see them profess true faith at young ages. That is supposed to be the natural process: all through Scripture, God speaks in terms of generational spiritual training and blessings. Parents are supposed to bring their children to a saving knowledge of the Lord, by His grace. Our Lord pointed out that children have a simple, but wonderful faith—so wonderful that we as adults are to have faith like a child. Why did He say this about children? Because it is so natural (read: God-ingrained) for them to imitate and trust their parents. That trust for his parents forms the basis for the child's trusting the Heavenly Father and, by extension, His salvation in Jesus Christ. Certainly children and adults often are saved outside the home, and sometimes even in spite of a lousy home, but Scripture still maintains that the home is *supposed* to be the primary place children learn about and come to salvation.

Do our Christian schools, generally speaking, structure their teaching on salvation in line with Scripture? Or do these schools take the parents' role upon themselves, with the parents tacit or even stated acquiescence? Just because parents may not mind or even (mistakenly) consider abdicating a good thing in any area, that does not make it okay for the school to comply. Am I saying that Christian schools should not teach children about salvation? May it never be! But too many schools lose sight of who is do be the *primary* teacher and intermediary for a child's coming to the Father. Instruction in the Bible and its precepts should be a hallmark of any Christian school, but clever songs, recitations of Scripture, posters, even memorized creeds, while good in themselves, should not be treated as a means of grace for the salvation of students.[†]

Strange as it may sound, teachers in a Christian school should very rarely pray with a student to become a Christian. In those rare instances, even non-believing parents should be involved as quickly as possible. Once the foundation of grace and belief has been laid in the student's life from a second birth at home, the Christian school should be ready and equipped to systematically and practically teach and help build that new faith with regular, sound biblical instruction throughout a well-planned curriculum.

Other, less critical but still important areas where parental abdication may be tolerated or fostered often include:

1. Involvement: Does the school have virtually countless ways and levels for parents to be actively involved in the day-

---

[†] A slight tangent here: could someone please explain to me the scriptural defense of a "salute" to the "Christian" flag or to the Bible? I just don't get it.

to-day work, or are parents tacitly encouraged to just drop off the kid and the tuition check?

2. Evaluation: Does the school take every opportunity possible to inform the parents about the instructional aspects of the school, any changes in curriculum, the goals and philosophy of the school, *etc.*, and about how parents may evaluate and give input on the school's work? Or are parents treated like customers in an auto repair shop: "Yeah, we'll take care of that 'clunking sound', lady. Just give us the keys and have a seat."

3. Discipline: Does the school assume or preempt the family's role of being the initial place children learn to respect authority? Is Dad recognized as the critical contact and shaper of the children's discipline? In some cases I rarely see the dad. Little Johnny's been in my office and I've called up the dad with, "Hi, this is Tom Garfield," to hear "Who?" Nevertheless, though Mom may want to do it, Dad is the one who is supposed to provide the discipline.

4. Some related topics: Sex education and drug/alcohol abuse programs: Why not do this for the parents? Because the school is assuming it can *inculcate* morals, while the job of a Christian school is to *reinforce* morals. Those areas involve primary moral decisions. In the drug-hazed, 'just say yes' days of the sixties, I just said "no" because I knew my parents would be disappointed and hurt. Schools, even good Christian ones, can't teach the students to make those moral choices, only the parents can.

I haven't seen a Christian school yet that doesn't say it supports the family. But could they support the family in their policies and procedures? Could they show someone that commitment by their day-to-day practices? Do we know where the lines are?

The Classical School and Caesar

Of primary importance here is a respect for the state's biblical role. What do we teach about the state? In this context, the "state" refers to the established civil government—local, state, and particularly, national. In our culture, considering the sorry state of our government, it is easy to be cynical and present a hopeless picture of the future to our students. This is not only a poor way to teach, it is unbiblical. Particularly and uniquely in the United States we are blessed with an incredibly Bible-rich history of our government. The students need to know, for their sakes and future generations' that our Constitution, for instance, was created following biblical principles, and constructed largely by intelligent, Christian men.

We must teach our students what the Bible says about the state, not what our culture, the Supreme Court or the media tells us about the state. We should teach them the history of where our government came from, and what has happened to it, as well as comparing it to other governments in the world today and other past civilizations. From the Levitical laws to Romans 13, the Scriptures are clear about the primary function of any governing authority, *i.e.*, it is God's servant to propagate moral (in conformity with His character) laws that enforce justice and provide protection for the citizenry. (Sounds almost like the preamble to the U.S. Constitution, doesn't it? No coincidence there.) In the famous passage in Matthew, Jesus' simple comment about "render to Caesar" could comprise enough material for a good portion of a decent civics course. Our Lord's judgement teaches us something about authority, civil structures, economics, and the responsibility of citizens, even in a corrupt, immoral state such as Rome was at the time of Christ. One obvious and very relevant aspect from Jesus' statement is that there are areas and functions that are under Caesar's jurisdiction (even if for a short time and delegated to him by the Father) and other areas and functions that are strictly God's alone. It would greatly behoove us as Christian educators to determine, from other revealed wisdom, which are which. For a good beginning, we may render to Caesar that which has his image on it. But if something has God's image on it, *as our children do*, they may not be "rendered to Caesar," but rather to God.

We would not, as educators, stop teaching proper English grammar to our students, just because English is abused and misused even by the popular, public orators of our culture. We should be equally diligent to present the foundations and purposes of good civil government to our students, in spite of, or more appropriately, because of the fact that we currently live under a corruption of sound governmental principles. Cynicism and defeatism are practiced by the pagans. Christians and Christian educators should be equipped to not just realize the darkness is a curse, but to know what true light is. Students should grow up knowing that not only did God ordain the current authorities in their present positions, these students should know how to recognize and, Lord willing, be able to implement godly governments.

A good place to start educating students about the role of the state is by insisting on biblical standards of conduct in school, from kindergarten on up. Good discipline in the school teaches the kids about the state operating as it should, *i.e.*, citizens respecting a just magistrate, and abiding by biblically-patterned laws. As mentioned above, a student's respect for and obedience to principles of right and wrong must begin in the home, as God designed. It cannot and will not begin at school. Even a five-year old child, as the Word says, "is known by his deeds, whether they are right and pure" (Prov. 20:11). And even a five-year old who is unruly can be a major problem for a teacher and a class full of kids.

As students grow in their ability to understand both the history and purpose of biblical governments, it will become increasingly obvious to them that something has gone wrong with our state. So, from a well-constructed historical and biblical foundation, the students should be taught that indeed, some things have gone radically wrong. Our state has jumped out of its domain and has trespassed into the God-ordained domains of the family and the church. The state blatantly trespasses into the realm of the family by trying to morally guide and educate the children. It has trespassed more subtly into the domain of the church by trying to feed and clothe the poor, and redeem (*vs.* simply punishing) the wrongdoer. It takes little astuteness to see that it has failed miserably to succeed in either area of trespass.

The state's role is *not* to teach the family. Its role is not to replace the church and certainly it is not to keep the church at bay by using strong-armed legalities to enforce the myth of "separation of church and state." The state is designed to protect the family and the church so that they can perform their God-ordained duties, without fear of harassment, and without fear of abuse or interference from evil men.

We Have Not Come To Praise Caesar's Schools

Christian schools, like many Christian churches, often assume they began when their doors opened. A logical enough assumption. But ideas, good or bad, always precede consequences. Christian and classical schools need to know not only historically whence they came, but we also need to remember how our current government schools evolved. If we forget or don't know where we originated, we will certainly lose sight of where we're headed. And if we don't know or forget where the government schools came from, we are far more likely to fall into the pit they dwell in today.

For a sad example, recently I had a call from a Christian school board member in southern Idaho. Her school began just about five years ago. However, the founding visionaries of the school left rather quickly after the school's inception, and her call to me had to do with the school's serious consideration of going after state accreditation. How could something begun so well get so off track so fast? If the question comes to your mind, "What's so awful about state accreditation?", you either don't know your history and/or your Bible well enough. Others have done a far better and more thorough summary of the state's encroachment on education than

I have time or expertise to repeat here. A brief overview is therefore all I will attempt. May it serve to illustrate the point that the state is a poor surrogate teacher.

From Karl Marx to Horace Mann to John Dewey to the current proponents of state-supplied ("It's the American, democratic way") education, the common thread among secular educators is the belief that man is basically good and only needs to be educated away from evil. Marx, the designer of the failed communist state, proposed as part of his manifesto that the state supply "free, public education" for all children, in order to have a subservient, orderly citizenry. (To be fair, most public education advocates aren't aware of this strong connection to communistic thought.) Then, in the middle of the nineteenth century, a Massachusetts man named Horace Mann, enamored with the new ideas coming out of Europe, advocated not only "free public education", but also *mandatory* education for all children. Parents didn't always insist that their children get the kind of education that a society needs its citizenry to have, Mann believed, so the state must force the parents to do the "right" thing. The next step was obvious—this "free" education would be paid for by taxing Paul to allow Peter to go to school. Mann firmly and sincerely believed in the messianic possibilities of a "free" public education. The schools will provide a means for shutting down the jails. He really believed that and said "we will empty our jails." An educated society would by deduction be a godly society.

John Dewey is called the father of public education. He advocated and got many of his ideas put into place in the government schools back in the 30's. He had ideas very similar to Mann, only he wasn't quite so altruistic. Mann at least said it'd be a good thing for people to be good. He had a sense of right and wrong. Dewey basically said we need to mold children, we need to shape their minds to make them good citizens of the state and the way to do that is in the classroom. He was an active contributor to the first Humanist

Manifesto. Dewey had an extremely low regard for the family, and for its role in education.

Finally, under the administration of FDR in the thirties and forties, the state was seen, for the first time in our history, as the benevolent care-provider and citizen maker. The decade after his death, the fifties, saw the social-engineering U.S. Supreme Court under chief justice Earl Warren change the face of public schools through active intrusion. Under the excuse of morally cleansing the schools of segregation, the Warren Court set the stage for the fatal blow—making Bible-reading and prayer illegal in the public schools after 1963. While granting the system was an aberration anyway, this final act removed the basis for any consistent form of learning or discipline in these schools. Decades later, charts illustrating the rise in illiteracy and juvenile delinquency all skyrocket up from that point in time.

This is the state system that vast numbers of Christian schools look to for approval of their programs, programs supposedly based on the Scriptures. They are rendering to Caesar the things that are God's.

State Accreditation vs. Excellence in Education

Frequently, when I interview new families, one of the parents asks about our accreditation status with the state. It is also very common that they inquire about the certification requirements we place upon our teaching applicants. These are understandable questions, given the conditioning to which we, as a culture, have been subject. We have been told, both directly and subliminally, that state accreditation is to education what the FDA stamp of approval is to food quality, *i.e.,* the guarantee of rigorous scrutiny by knowledgeable experts. The only problem is that if the FDA's stamp indicated the same "quality" in food that state accreditation does for schools, salmonella and hepatitis would be as common as the cold and we'd all resort to raising our own food. Not too surprisingly, many people have done just that in education; they've started their own schools!

The idea of holding educational institutions and their instructors accountable and ensuring they maintain high standards is very appropriate. However, at least two things need to be carefully considered:

1. *Who* or *what* is the superior and responsible agency to which the institution is accountable?

2. *What standards* are used as the yardstick against which the institution is being measured?

It's very disappointing to me to see so many Christians become schizophrenic (Greek—"split mind") on this issue. On most other issues involving children and their training, most Christians resort immediately to the Scriptures. To cut to the chase, the Bible clearly and without apology says parents are the primary educators. They are the "*who*" to which any institution educating children must be accountable. The state has been given no biblical authority in education. Doesn't it then follow that the "*standards*" are also up to the parents, within certain, specified biblical guidelines?

If this isn't convincing enough, consider two other points—has state accreditation consistently bequeathed us better and better educated citizens, or just the opposite? Further, the actual accreditation process gives barely a nod to the academic performance of a school's students. Instead, it majors on the physical plant and faculty numbers. At Logos we not only believe we operate directly under the collective authority of our families (as verbalized and channeled by our board), a large percentage of our staff is comprised of parents. The standards we hold all our staff members to, and the school at large, come from the Bible. Therefore, loving the children and modeling the Christian life to them are enforced standards.

In the end, the excellence of any education is discerned

by the quality evidenced in the lives of the students, not by state-approved, meaningless certificates.

Some Final Danger Zones

Our federal "Caesar" has grown to wield so much power and influence that even Augustus would turn chartreuse with envy, were he alive to witness it. No longer is the government, or more accurately, are government agencies satisfied to regulate and control their own schools, private education is now virtually under siege. While prayerfully avoiding the temptation to fear, Christian schools should nonetheless be alert to the actions and plans of the forces guiding lawmakers.

Unless someone has been living in the heart of Antarctica for the last decade or two, we are all aware of the litigious nature of our current culture. This includes a great increase of lawsuits brought against Christian schools, by people from within and without those schools. From hiring practices to discipline standards to causes for dismissal, Christian schools need to be sure their written policies and bylaws are adequate to meet the spirit of the age. Legal advice from a Christian lawyer who is familiar with potential problems should be a useful avenue to take advantage of as needed. The state is rarely sympathetic to the concerns near and dear to Christian educators, and so the old standard of being forearmed applies to Christian schools as never before.

Another area of potential state encroachment and/or harassment is that brought through the accepting of federal or state monies by Christian schools. To put it bluntly, Christian schools should not accept money from anyone or anything, unless there is clearly no tether attached. Any and all monies "granted" by the state should be regarded as having the equivalent of the Titanic's anchor chain clamped firmly to them, with the same wonderful fate awaiting that school as happened to that ship.

Finally, beware the agencies of the state: health, taxation, child protection services, welfare, OSHA (safety), and even transportation, to name a few. The best idea is a low profile, don't wave red flags drawing the state's attention to the school. Obviously as Christians we should do even more than the pagans in caring for and protecting our precious children through facility safety and cleanliness. But the state has a whole different idea and agenda for taking care of our kids. Common sense, and certainly scriptural guidelines play little part in what the state considers good for children. Again, being informed about the basic essentials seems to be the wisest road to follow. Asking questions of too many bureaucrats not only will confuse the school administration, it will possibly encourage the bureaucrat's office to pass along other ridiculous "guidelines." Always remember that a bureaucrat's regulations do not necessarily have the force of law, even though *he* may believe that they do.

Classical schools, as a subset of Christian schooling, should lead the way in modeling right, biblical thinking and acting by respecting the governments God has established. At times that will mean treating those governments—family, church, and state—in ways they are not expecting or used to. Therefore, seeking godly discernment and a constant study of God's Word are prerequisites and continuing requirements for any Christian educator.

NINETEEN:

In Loco Parentis
Tom Spencer

Let us start with a test question, open book. Where in Scripture does God give authority to schools to teach and train children? List chapter and verse. Stumped? This raises a question worth considering. Where do schools get the authority to do what they do? Most people today believe that education is the responsibility of the state governments. They say that schools receive their authority from the state governments. The federal government would like to get their hands in the pie as well. What does Scripture say?

> Hear, O Israel: The Lord our God, the Lord is one. Love the Lord your God with all your heart and with all your soul and with all your strength. These commandments that I give you today are to be upon your hearts. Impress them on your children. Talk about them when you sit at home and when you walk along the road, when you lie down and when you get up (Deuteronomy 6:4-9).

In this passage, God is not addressing governments or schools, God is addressing *parents*. Let us look at a second biblical passage that addresses the teaching of children.

> Children, obey your parents in the Lord, for this is right. 'Honor your father and mother'—which is the first commandment with a promise—'that it may go well with you and that you may enjoy long life on the earth.' Fathers, do

237

not exasperate your children; instead, bring them up in the training and instruction of the Lord (Ephesians 6:1-4).

These verses share an obvious similarity; both indicate that God gives the authority for teaching children to parents. Where then do schools get their authority to teach children? Before examining the source of the school's authority, it is important to note that it does not come directly from God.

Historically, schools have operated from the legal notion of *in loco parentis*. According to this concept, parents temporarily delegate their authority to school officials during the day. This idea has a long history. For example, Blackstone (1723-1780) wrote that a parent,

> . . . may . . . delegate part of his parental authority, during his life, to the tutor or schoolmaster of his child; who is then *in loco parentis*, and has such a portion of the power of the parent committed to his charge, *viz.* that is restraint and correction, as may be necessary to answer the purposes for which he is employed.[1]

Although it is not the primary focus of this essay, notice how compulsory attendance laws have obliterated this historic legal doctrine. Legislators have passed laws based on a non-biblical assumption, namely, that the government, not the parents, is responsible for the education of children. The United States Supreme Court has upheld this revision. In *Ingraham v. Wright*, 430 U.S. 651, 662 (1977), the Supreme Court stated,

> "The concept of parental delegation" as a source of school authority is not entirely "consonant with compulsory education laws".[2]

---

[1] Blackstone, *Commentaries on the Laws of England*, as quoted in Arval A. Morris, *The Constitution and American Public Education* (Durham, NC: Carolina Academic Press, 1989), p. 277.

[2] *Ibid.*, p. 278.

School administrators, board members, and teachers must be aware of the philosophical basis from which the government schools operate today. Compulsory attendance laws are based on a non-biblical premise. Yet many of our assumptions about the proper role of the school are based on our personal experience attending these schools. We need to re-examine the proper role of the school from a biblical basis.

Christian schools receive delegated authority from the parents. This authority is the basis for their actions. When schools design their program, they do not need to try to meet the expectations of every parent. Schools must work with tens and hundreds of different parents. Each set of parents represents a slightly different collection of standards. Satisfying every parent all of the time is not possible. Rather, schools should establish principles for their academic, discipline, and extracurricular programs. These principles will reflect the educational philosophy of the school. Once they have expressed these principles *clearly* to the parents, it is up to the parents to decide whether they support the established program or not. Practically speaking, a school of any size cannot establish many independent programs. That is not a strength of a formal classroom setting. It follows that not all parents will choose your program for their children. This is to be expected.

Those who draft academic standards must build recognition of parental authority into the policy structure. They must be careful in the construction of our policies to acknowledge, and not undermine, the authority of parents. If we are not careful, we can draft policies common to government schools without realizing that the policies work against parental responsibility. Let us look at some practical issues facing schools as they attempt to establish their academic program.

Parental responsibility affects the admissions process. Before accepting a student for enrollment in your school, you must meet the parents. Administrators need to determine how parents view their role. Parents seem to fall into two categories concerning this issue. First, there are parents who understand their God given responsibility to train and educate their children. There are also parents who either do not understand this idea or have abdicated their responsibility. It would be a great mistake for a school to attempt to fill in for abdicating parents. They have no authority to do so. How can you tell what type of parent you are dealing with? Ask the parents what they expect from the school. Ask them why they want to enroll their child in your school. Listen carefully to their responses. Find out what their expectations are. They may not be able to articulate a biblical answer, chapter and verse. Still, do their actions show that they are fulfilling their responsibility? Are the parents looking for a partner or a surrogate parent? If the parents want to pass their mantle of responsibility to you, you would be wise to avoid admitting their children into your school.

Impressing new school administrators and faculty members with the importance of this issue is difficult. The success of your educational program will, in large part, depend upon it. Do not fool yourself into thinking that what you do at school will overcome a poor situation at home; it will not. The child's life at home is the foundation upon which you will be building.

When will you need parental support? The answer is more times than you can probably imagine. You will need it when Johnny is misbehaving in class. You will need it when Susie is struggling to learn to read. Older students will not accept the philosophy of classical and Christian education if their parents do not. I recently reviewed some application materials developed at Cair Paravel Latin School in Topeka, Kansas. It was clear from the design and structure of the application form that the administrators at Cair Paravel knew from experience just how important this issue is. The application informs the parents of many particulars and distinctives of the Cair Paravel program. There is no hidden agenda. They describe the academic program in detail. I suspect many people who request an application form decide not to return it, and that is good. They have not designed the Cair Paravel program for every student. Yet those parents who do enroll their children at Cair Paravel know the philosophy of education on which the academic program is based. They also know what role Cair Paravel expects parents to play in their children's education.

One of the most critical ways that schools acknowledge their respect for parents is by frequent and timely communication from the teachers. Have you ever heard a parent lament that they received too much information from the school about their children? Is a child struggling academically? The teacher should inform the parents. Is the child misbehaving? The teacher should inform the parents. Did the student ask to have the gospel shared with them or seek counseling from a teacher? The school should inform the parents. Timely communication shows that the school knows who is the boss.

At Logos School, we have developed several policies and guidelines to ensure that parents receive critical information on a regular basis. At the elementary level, each teacher sends home a weekly note. The parents receive information about the student's behavior during the week. Teachers also notify parents about upcoming tests and homework assignments. Parents with elementary and secondary students will receive at least eight academic reports during the school year; four midterm reports and four report cards. Each of these items includes a space for parents to write a response to the teachers or administrators. We schedule formal parent-teacher conferences twice a year. We also notify parents at least two weeks before the end of a grading period if their child is in danger of failing a class. Taken together, this represents a *minimum* level of communication from school to parent.

Parental responsibility affects the academic program in many ways. Schools hire teachers to assist the parents as they fulfill their God given responsibility. Each class is made up of students with a variety of abilities. God has not made all children equal, some are smarter and learn more quickly than others. In each class, there will probably be some students who are struggling academically. Most often this results from poor study habits or not paying attention in class. Sometimes, the program may be too challenging for the child. Whatever the cause, eventually the teacher will need to contact the parents to express their concern for the student. If the school and the parents understand their responsibilities, they will work together to meet the needs of the student. The teacher will receive support from the parents. The parents will help the teachers to understand the character, needs, and abilities of their child. This is the chief benefit of parent-teacher conferences. A teacher may have a concern about a student and ask the parents for advice on how to handle the situation. Whatever the particular situation, a major part of finding a solution will be to contact the parents. Another indication of the school's view of parents is the way they respond to parents' requests for information. Parents should receive timely responses to their requests for information.

Another related academic situation occurs when a student enters the school and finds himself unable to keep up with the academic pace at the school. This is common for older students. It may result from deficiencies in their earlier education. In such a case, who is responsible for helping the students to catch up? The school is certainly responsible for helping the student in mastering the current work, but the parents must accept the responsibility for helping the student catch up. This may require that the parents give their children additional tutoring, or hire a tutor for their son or daughter. There is a distinct difference between the work of the parents and the work of the school.

Discipline is another area that requires schools and parents to work together. One of the most serious consequences students at Logos School receive is a formal office visit. This involves the teacher bringing the student to meet with the principal for a serious offense such as cheating, swearing, fighting, showing disrespect to a staff member, *etc.* Because of the office visit, the students will receive some type of discipline; a spanking for an elementary student; perhaps restitution for a secondary student. An integral part of this policy requires the administrator to contact the parents following the office visit. The administrator must inform the parents about the offense and the discipline. The school board built this process on one premise. It assumes that the parents will support the discipline meted out at the school. If the school and parents agree on the nature of the offense and the discipline given, the discipline will be effective and the student will benefit. If the parents do not support the school's discipline, the process breaks down. What if the parent disagrees with the discipline given by the administrator? Sometimes this will happen. The administrator should be willing to change his decision, although he may still believe he was right. The parents may tell the student that the administrator has changed his decision because the parents do not agree. In this situation, the administrator should ask that the parents decide upon the discipline. Being able to continue to work together is vital for the parents and administrator. It is more important than it is for the administrator to stick to his decision and have a disgruntled parent.

Attendance policies and guidelines are one area in which the needs of the school programs and the rights of the parents may conflict. Schools rely upon the regular attendance of the students. However, parents should always have the right to have their child miss school for a day, or even a week, if they think that is best. Attendance policies should not prohibit parents from going on vacation during the school year. The school should not create a policy under which an administrator has to judge the merits of the absence, *i.e.,* deciding between excused and unexcused absences. (I am not referring to a student who misses class without his parent's permission.) Schools however, should determine how to work with parental desires while maintaining the integrity of the academic program. This is a difficult balancing act.

Given the tremendous God-given responsibilities of parenthood, schools should not take more than their share of the blame when students fail, either academically or behaviorally. The best school cannot overcome weaknesses in the home. Along the same line of reasoning, schools should be careful not to take too much credit for students who are successful. Schools again have the advantage of building on strong foundations in the lives of successful students. This thinking should temper the evaluations of the school's failures and successes. School personnel should avoid the extremes of pride and despair when they evaluate their program. Keep this in mind when you review your standardized test scores, and when students leave your school for another.

Finally, if you want to take a reading on how well the school understands the role of the parents, observe how the school treats parents who visit the school. Are parents welcomed into the classrooms, even when they arrive without notice? They should be. We should treat parents like VIPs because, after all, they are. I remember the story of one school where one parent wanted to be able to help in her daughter's first grade classroom. The teacher refused to allow the mother into the room; it would be too distracting to the students. Finally, after a great deal of persistence, the mother was allowed to help the teacher. The teacher allowed her to read to small groups of students, in the hallway! The teacher did not allow her into the classroom. Not surprisingly, the mother was soon looking for a new school for her daughter. Parents should know that they are always welcome to visit the school. We have one mother who visits secondary classrooms weekly. Admittedly, sometimes this can make the teachers nervous, but we all respect the parent for taking their responsibilities seriously. We only wish that all parents were as diligent to check on the training their children are receiving. The Supreme Court may think that the doctrine of *in loco parentis* is passe, but it should be alive and well in your school.

TWENTY:

Practical Steps in Starting a School
Tom Garfield

Disclaimer

Goodly numbers of sizable books by well-experienced authors have been written on this topic, or at least very similar material. It is simply impossible in a chapter's length to examine every critical area related to getting something started that is as big and important as a classical, Christian school. For instance, curriculum selection will have to be just lightly touched on, due to the many intricacies it entails. However, as long as the reader understands the inherent limitations, and if the areas examined below save the reader at least a modicum of trouble, the author will be genuinely pleased.

First Considerations, *or*
Why in the World Would You Want to Do This?

Determining your motivations for even considering such a scheme is of utmost and primary concern. Very seriously speaking, if you take the plunge and commit to building a school, you (and all those you involve in the first steps) will repeatedly ask the above question: "Why in the world are we doing this?" The first flush of excitement, like that of romance, will fade quickly, and there had better be real substance beneath the feelings. Below are some questions to probe for the presence of that necessary, substantive foundation.

What percent, approximately, of your primary motivations for wanting a classical school are reactionary and what percent are reasoned? As the saying goes, you could throw a rock with your eyes shut and hit a reason to leave the government schools. There are explicit and implicit problems galore. Over the years of hearing parents' reasons for seeking to enroll their students at Logos, two motivational categories have emerged. One is what I would call reactionary—"We can't stand the public schools because of X, so we want to try something else." The other category is reasoned—"We have come to the conclusion that we want our children educated biblically, and are seeking the best way to do that."

Obviously, there are mixes of the two motivations, e.g., parents who come to biblical convictions about education at the same time they become disenchanted with the public schools. That may be your situation as well. All the more reason then to determine how much of each motivation you are relying on to keep you going through the work ahead. Reactions wear off, and a condition somewhat akin to the Israelites wanting to go back to Egypt can set in, "Gee, it wasn't that bad back there, after was it? It's really hard right now and maybe we should consider turning around and seeing if Pharaoh (or the NEA) has had a change of heart." Only having convictions like Moses' can keep you going through the wilderness.

Will you be building for real children or hypothetical ones? Now that sounds rather odd, on the surface. That question is not referring to enrollment, either. Certainly you need to build with future, larger numbers of students in mind. That's just good planning. No, what the question is referring to is your understanding of the nature, interests, sins, characteristics, ages, gender differences, and abilities of the smaller portion of our species, i.e., children. Do you know any children? Do your potential teachers know any? I mean, really well? If not, there is a tendency or temptation to start a school with one or more of the following erroneous presumptions about your students:

1. By just applying the tried and true classical method, we will produce mostly geniuses after just a few years.

2. Kids from Christian homes, especially those that enroll in our school, will need very little, if any, discipline from us.

3. Parents of our students will unfailingly support the school and its teachers.

4. The kids will love the school and be naturally kind to each other, even on the playground.

5. Children by the ripe old age of kindergarten will be able to assimilate Latin, Greek, and simple calculus equations.

6. Our students will eagerly want to learn, especially in *our* ideal setting.

There are other presumptions that will lead to real disappointments as well. That is, they will disappoint you unless you trot them out and look at them in the light of reality. Ideas are not enough, you must study children and plan your school and program accordingly.

What about your broad, or long term, vision? The Scriptures say without vision, a people perish. Vision is not a reaction. It is an idea or picture of the future, as someone would like to see it implemented. But your vision for your school is going to need far more substance than that. Before anyone entrusts their children to your care, from this point on, they will want to know some basic things about your vision. Such as:

1. What will make your school different from the government schools, and more importantly, from other Christian schools?

2. What in the world is this "classical" business all about, anyway?

3. What will the graduates from your school be like?

4. What qualifications will you require of your teachers and staff members?

5. How do you plan to achieve these lofty, idealistic goals?

This is an extremely abbreviated list of potential questions. Before your doors open for the first time, you will likely be required to answer hundreds more. C.S. Lewis once said that an idea is not truly great unless it can be summed up on the back of a postcard. That means someone has to be able to articulate it, and do so succinctly, meaningfully, and repeatedly. Actually, virtually every key person in the formation of the school needs to be able to articulate the vision in this way. While many schools can start (as Logos did) with the singular vision of primarily one man, few can get far without that vision being caught and understood by many others. It just takes a lot of people to do the job and do it well.

So, the second part of knowing your vision is to consider: Who shares, or might share, your vision? Far from being alone, as you might be tempted to feel at times, there are many people who are already sharing your ideas, you all just need to get together and find out who the "others" are. How to do that? Stick close to home, don't look far afield for co-visionaries. Long distances make school planning very difficult. Be bold: actively announce your desire to meet with like-minded believers in your church, or other solid scriptural churches in the area, to discuss the ramifications of a classical, Christian school, and your vision for it.

You will quickly notice, once the group begins gathering and talking on a regular basis, that two basic groups will emerge, divided somewhat by gender lines, but not strictly. There will be the natural visionaries, the "Hey-I've-got-an-idea!" types. These will mostly be men, probably men who don't work with their hands a lot. Then there will be the administrative worriers, the "Where-are-we-going-to-get-the-desks?" types. These will possibly be women, or men who like to organize their workbenches. Both types (and genders) are needed in this critical planning stage. Without the visionaries, the transcontinental railroad would never have been dreamed of and we would have been a country divided east and west (instead of north and south). But without the administrators, the railroad would have probably connected up somewhere in Saskatoon.

So, What Will You Use As a Foundation?

You must have as your all-encompassing, highest priority your philosophy of Christian education. Like your vision, this will touch on everything you do, or rather, everything you do will reflect your philosophy. It differs from your vision in the same way the road differs from the destination. The philosophy, if well-developed, will be a reliable path, which (to extend the metaphor) will broaden and strengthen with definition over time to become a heavy-duty, four-lane, smooth highway to safely speed your students toward your vision for them. Neat, huh?

In light of this volume of collected works, we will assume you will have a philosophy of education that is rooted deeply in the classical and Christian foundation. Therefore, it is not necessary or propitious to examine this philosophy in depth here. The reader is referred to other readings for a good examination of the nature of this philosophy.[1]

However, there are other overall considerations that will pertain to the basic, scriptural applications of your philosophy. Here we consider the application of scriptural authority in the school, and some related foundational questions:

1. Will the school be church-run? If so, who makes up the governing board, and how is the family's scriptural authority viewed and appropriated? Churches are often closely associated with schools, if not in complete control of them, usually for two basic reasons. First, there is a strong, like-minded consensus among the church families, resulting in a more homogeneous school environment, administration, and direction. Secondly, the church already has a completed,

---

[1] See Douglas Wilson, *Recovering the Lost Tools of Learning* (Wheaton, IL: Crossway Books, 1991).

school-friendly facility. It makes financial sense to appropriate and consolidate common resources.

There are pitfalls to both of those reasons, the most obvious being that though people may attend the same church, they may indeed have very different educational goals for their children and their children's school. But a church-run school can be done well, in theory. The key is to check how the family's authoritative role is recognized, and *functionally acknowledged*.

2. Another option for the administrative structure is a family-run school. This sounds ideal, or at least vaguely scriptural, and runs something like this: every family in the school has to subscribe to a common statement of purpose, and participates fully in most or all major decisions related to the school. It is a form of direct democracy, and like that form of government, it is rarely used today. Reason? It can become rather unwieldy to operate. But again, it is *possible* to do, since a number of Christian schools continue to operate that way today.

3. Admittedly the administration of choice is a board-run structure. This allows for parents to actively serve in positions of administrative and directional authority, in more of a republican or representative style. But it is important for the board to remain true to the original vision of the school's founders, regardless of the various whims of parental pressure.

4. What about affiliations with the federal government agencies, the state, the local public school district, other educational organizations—A.C.S.I., A.C.C.S, A.S.C.D., N.H.S., *etc.*? As with all relationships, cautious diplomacy is necessary. Caution should include a full examination of the benefits and concerns inherent with any relationship.[2]

------

[2] See chapter 18 in this book which addresses state accreditation.

For many of the questions related to this area, that is, associated *advisory* institutions, the bottom line is: Where will you turn for answers to philosophical questions? Obviously the Scriptures are the primary source of wisdom, but what will be your source for applied, practical wisdom? Other, secondary sources will prove to be helpful, too.

Having this next step in place will greatly assist you in determining who your "friends" are. Your mission statement and school goals, based on your philosophy, will determine the direction of the entire school program in very practical ways. It will be these goals, from which policies and guidelines are developed, that your administrator will look to for his compass heading. Also from these documents your curriculum objectives can be determined and evaluated. The goals and mission statement need to be broad enough to set standards for many years of work, but they also need to be specific enough to clarify your school's unique approach to education. For example, "We will seek to train the students to be good citizens" sounds very nice and wholesome, but does it reflect your unique philosophy well, on the one hand, and, on the other hand, does it give the administration and teachers enough guidance to build the program? The USSR in its heyday no doubt trained students to be "good citizens!" At the risk of sounding self-serving, Logos School has developed goals that have provided broad standards, and yet have been specific enough to give guidance to the school staff for over fifteen years. It can be done well.

Another consideration is what you will consider the means you will use to implement your vision will be the school's program structure. This is not the facility, but it will greatly affect your facility, as well as curricular, decisions. (You will notice that the actual facilities haven't been addressed yet. That's because we are going by priority, and they just don't matter as much as these other items.)

In deciding your program's structure and scope, your choices will either assist or hinder your vision. Again, your stated philosophy will be your best guide. Some options you may want to consider are: K-6, K-8, P-6, 1-6, 7-12, 7-9, K-12, P-12. (P=Preschool, K=Kindergarten for five-year-olds.) Will you have a daycare program included in your school? Daycares are usually done because they are almost always a cash cow, or money-maker, for the school. But that is a *poor* motivation for implementing such a program. Rather, will it really fulfill part of your vision?

Unless your school will be in a setting with an established network of other good Christian schools, a full P- or K-12 program is strongly recommended. Considering the goals and strengths of a classical education, truncating the process at any point is simply illogical. However, as soon as you let it be known that your group will be attempting a high school program, there will be many nay-sayers who will do their best to scare you off. Stick to your guns. The high school will be extremely expensive and hard to do, but very worth all the labor you put into it.

Then, related to the program's structure and scope is the choice of classroom structures:

1. What will be your ideal student:teacher ratio? How will you work toward that, and once achieved, how will it be maintained?

2. Will you have combination (mixed level) classes? Very likely you will need to, at least for awhile, to make the most of your staff and finances. How many levels/grades will be in one class—two, three (gulp), . . . four? Check out the pros and cons, as well as tricks of the trade.

3. Will you stick to grouping the students by age level, *i.e.* similar in each grade, or will you group them by ability? Ability grouping can also be done, and can often be more manageable, within a classroom/grade.

Staffing Matters

Who will you put on the "front lines?" Before the first person (preferably your administrator) is hired, some critical decisions regarding staff need to be made.

First you must establish lines of authority: Who directs/serves whom? What will be the necessary documentation to illustrate and support those lines? For example, some kind of a written contract will be necessary—the days of hearty-hand-shakes-all-'round-and-that's-all-that's-necessary are long gone.

Secondly, you must consider accountability: How will you determine that staff members are all doing their jobs? Suggestion: make your job descriptions and evaluation tools parts of the same document.

Then you must consider qualifications: What will be needed by the teachers? Job descriptions, other documents identifying the spiritual, professional, philosophical, practical, and personal qualifications need to be constructed (or borrowed and adapted to your needs).

And of course there are many other practical issues. Just a few of the other more important policies to have in some form prior getting a staff together include: Recruiting, interviewing, checking references, hiring, salaries, training, retention, and dismissals/firing.

Your administrator will be the person who guides, oversees, leads, and wholeheartedly supports the teachers in their critical roles. Since he will be the only point person for your whole school, loads of thought and prayer need to go into this crucial hiring. Will you hire an administrator for your first year or try to go for it without one? (Strong recommendation—bite the financial bullet and get one right away. Your teachers will benefit greatly!) Will this person be male or female? Will that matter to you? (It should.) At the risk of being very unpolitically correct, it is recommended that you seek out a man, married preferably. Scriptural leadership will be necessary, and though there are very capable women administrators, God largely directs men to be leaders in settings such as this. Will this person be full- or part-time? Many schools find that a part-time administrator, who also teaches to make a full-time position is a good way to start. That is far preferable to not having one at all, or one who is not on campus all day in some capacity.

The administrator's job description and evaluation tool are extremely critical. Having one done up front, before anyone is hired is very important. It can get messy when a teacher needs to be corrected or fired; it can get downright destructive to the school itself when the administrator needs correction, or firing. Such is the vital nature of that position.

So, where will you find those brilliant, loving, sacrificing, committed people to teach and work in your school? That query is probably in the top two questions that we get asked at Logos School. There are many sources to check out. Believe it or not, the better you know what you're looking for and wanting them to do, the more likely it is that you will find the right people. Here are some sources, in recommended order of contact and advertisement:

a. Parent constituency: possibly your best staffing resource.

b. Local churches that you trust.

c. A.C.C.S. contacts.

d. A.C.S.I. listings.

e. *World* magazine listings.

Some Final Considerations

You need to consider the importance of recruiting/accepting students. Much could be said about this, and has been, so this will be brief. From our experience, the bottom line is this: Advertising serves the purpose of keeping your school's name before the public eye and mind; a necessary and good idea, but it will not directly bring in students. Students will come if their parents trust other parents who trust you. This is called word-of-mouth, and it is hands-down the best recruiting tool you will *not* be able to directly use. But if you do your job right, "they will come." Your admissions policy and practices will have an immense effect on the atmosphere and functioning, not to mention reputation, of your school. "Choose wisely!"

Assuming you will have students, what will you do with them? Here is a list of various and sundry considerations that will need to be nailed down and distributed: discipline means far more than just a spanking. Your school rules should be founded on, but not equal to, God's rules. Your class rules should be simple, few, and similar. You need to have discipline policies which address procedures, parent involvement, and the biblical foundations.

You also must consider your dress code—what it will be, and how it will be enforced. Uniforms are a good idea, but insist on them from the beginning. Don't try to institute uniforms later.

When you establish school programs, choose wisely— what you start will become tradition quickly. With extracurricular programs, only do what you can do well.

With regard to your academic program, base it on your philosophy. Borrow a model, and don't buy any one publisher's complete program. Adapt and season your materials to your taste, as desired. Once you have your initial curriculum guide, then look at smaller, specialized publishers. You also need to have standards for lesson planning, homework, grading, testing (in-class and standardized), and reporting, as well as promotion and retention standards.

Facility and Finances

Finally we come to the mundane but critically necessary areas of finances and facilities. With regard to finances, assume there are no easy answers. First determine what you must do, and then determine what you want to do, and build budgets for both. Revenue will determine which budget you will be able to use.

Payroll is and must be the largest item: pay as much as you can and go up from there (consider the standard of living in the area). Curriculum materials are your next priority, and then after that, facility/overhead costs. Do the best you can with your materials; don't get cheap texts/materials for the kids. If you need to go cheap anywhere, go cheap on the facility.

Establish financially-related policies: setting fees (will they cover all the cost or will it be subsidized by gifts?), collecting revenue, setting budgets, paying bills, reporting, lines of management. Also establish your development office, which addresses PR, scholarships, and fund-raising.

With facilities: Keep it cheap, but make it look as good as possible. Churches are okay, but watch out for "political" entanglements. You don't want the pastor's wife trying to take over the curriculum committee. Keep the facility neat, clean, and safe. This will be necessary and it affects the school's effectiveness, morale, and reputation. If at all possible, avoid busing, but if you must, pay what you have to in order to keep the buses running safely and effectively. And watch out for government entanglements and regulations. Make facility plans and work toward them, all the while keeping your constituency fully informed.

What you are considering, or possibly have already recently begun, is one of the absolutely toughest tasks known to man—the effective training of the next generation. But since our Lord commanded it, He will provide the grace and strength you will need to do it. So plan to do it well, learn from your mistakes, where possible learn from others' mistakes, and saturate every decision and step with Scripture and prayer. He is faithful!

Epilogue:
The Rise and Fall of Government Education

Douglas Wilson

Horace Mann (1796-1858) was the father of the government schools in our country. He was deeply hostile to the historic Christian faith and sought to replace that faith with a "kinder, gentler faith," *i.e.*, a faith in man. It appears that historic Christianity had far too many sharp edges on which sinners might hurt themselves. The engine selected to propagate this humanistic faith was the common or "public" school. But as a true man of faith, Mann did not expect tiny things from his god. As he put it, "Let the Common School be expanded to its capabilities, let it be worked with the efficiency of which it is susceptible, and nine-tenths of the crimes in the penal code would become obsolete; the long catalogue of human ill would be abridged; men would walk more safely by day; every pillow would be more inviolable by night; property, life and character held by a stronger tenure; all rational hopes respecting the future brightened."[1]

But a century after the common schools were established, we are confronted with a dismal spectacle. It does not compare at all well with the glowing messianic vision for public education that was set forth by the seers and prophets of hu-

---

[1] As quoted in Rousas Rushdoony, *The Messianic Character of American Education* (Nutley, NJ: The Craig Press, 1963), p. 29.

manism in the last century. Astounding amounts of money
are being spent, academic standards have plummeted anyway,
and parents now have to worry about the physical safety of
their children. Many school officials have quit worrying about
gum under the seats and have started worrying about *guns*
under the seat, and whether the metal detectors at the doors
are adequate.

This poor outcome, however, should not have been such
a surprise to all of us. A few orthodox, thinking Christians of
the nineteenth century were not at all taken in. As mentioned
earlier, R.L. Dabney, a staff officer for "Stonewall" Jackson,
prophesied clearly where the attempt by the government to
provide a good, "neutral" education would all lead. He knew
what would happen to these government schools. "We have
seen that their complete secularization is logically inevitable.
Christians must prepare themselves then, for the following
results: All prayers, catechisms, and Bibles will ultimately be
driven out of the schools." A.A. Hodge, a great theologian at
Princeton, said that if the government schools were established, they would prove to be the greatest engine of atheism
the world had ever seen. Unfortunately, there were few Christians at that time with the insight of Dabney and Hodge.

This was because, although the intellectual impetus behind government schools was unbelieving and clearly humanistic, the local schools were still controlled at the local level
by Christians. Protestant evangelical Christians thought of
the public schools as "their" schools. The Roman Catholics
agreed with this, and began their parochial school system as a
response to the "evangelical" public schools. Only a few Christians had correctly identified the leaven of "neutrality," and
where it would lead us. It is hard to know what is more astonishing—those few Christians who saw the real issues a century ago, or those thousands of Christians today who still do
not see it.

The government schools were formed when the culture
of the United States was overwhelmingly and openly Chris-

tian. This is why some Christians today look back at those days with some degree of nostalgia. *If only* . . . If only we could return to the schools of the last century. If only we could return to McGuffy's Readers. Some of us wistfully look back to the government schools of our childhood, back before prayer was banned. *If only* . . . This nostalgic approach neglects one thing—the government schools were a rebellious idea from the start. Is it bad for the humanists to take our tax money and force us to educate our children according to a worldview we reject? But if it is bad for them to do this to us, then how was it good for us to do it to them? Parents are responsible for the education of their own children, and must not employ the coercive power of the state to educate the children of others. With regard to education, parents must determine its character, bear its costs, set its direction, and through what they do in their childrearing, present their children before God the Father at the last day. This is the law of God, and it is a law which cannot be obeyed through a civil magistrate who pretends that the existence of God is a matter of educational indifference. Education is one of the most religious things we do. The idea that it can be conducted from a "secular" vantage point is laughable. The pretense of neutrality can be made for a time, but only as a transitional tactic. When a culture is changing her gods, she usually cannot bear to jettison them all at once. She must be persuaded to do so gradually, and the farce of neutrality usually provides sufficient time and cover to do this.

Contrary to certain popular Christian assumptions, the crack-up of the government schools is not the result of them taking a "wrong turn" somewhere in the sixties. "We took God out of the schools, and look what happened." The god who was in the government schools before that time was an idol. It certainly made people who had little understanding of true religion feel good in praying to him, but this was only because this idol had all the divine characteristics and attributes of a celestial tapioca.

Christians must not be children in understanding; we must come to a mature mind. We must repent of our attempts to save "our" government schools. If the professing evangelical Christians in our nation were to take their children by their hands, and walk away, they would soon hear the roar of a collapsing and fallen god behind them. If they do not leave, it will still fall, but with their children inside.

Sorta Christian Academy

But leaving government education is not enough. Many Christian schools are almost as bad. Nevertheless, in the critique below no one school is in view; the critique addresses a composite school, which I am calling Sorta Christian Academy.

Sorta Christian Academy does not truly recognize the extent of our cultural crisis. While Sorta was founded in recognition of the fact that our secular culture and schools are falling apart, there is apparently little recognition that our evangelical culture has a case of the same disease—the modern church does not have an acknowledged epistemological center either. The Christian church at large is therefore in dire need of reformation according to the Scriptures and until that happens, most Christian schools, Sorta included, will continue to reflect the superficial nature of modern evangelical religion. Christian schools are a cultural manifestation of a particular Christian subculture. If that subculture is in an epistemic crisis of faith, the schools will reflect it. This is certainly the case at Sorta, where they do not see or understand the crisis in the church at large.

Sorta Christian Academy does not acknowledge the foundational educational role of parents. A successful Christian school is always an adjunct servant for successful Christian parents; it is not a replacement for them. But whenever a student succeeds at Sorta, the clear tendency is to claim that the school was the central shaping force in the student's life. In those situations where this is the case, it should be considered more an occasion for grief than anything else. And so

Sorta needs to act more like a servant school, and less like an orphanage; the Christian school is not a para-family organization, but rather a service for godly parents.

Sorta Christian Academy does not recognize the profound difference between a Christian school and a Christian church. The Christian school does not exist in order to conduct worship services, act as a mission agency, provide a mentoring and discipleship program for zealous young students, *etc.* The Christian school is not a church, or parachurch organization.

Sorta Christian Academy does not understand the fundamental antithesis between Christian culture and unbelieving culture. Consequently, most classes are taught in just the way they are taught in the government schools. The Christian element is "added" by means of a Bible class or chapel, as though God's truth were some kind of a condiment to spice up the autonomous food served up at the government schools. Thus, in most classes, the antithesis between light and dark is muddled. Does two and two make four whether God exists or not? When the average Christian cannot tell the answer, it is tragic; when the average teacher at a Christian school cannot tell you, it is inexcusable.

Sorta Christian Academy does not adequately distinguish between patriotism and faithfulness to Christ. Church history is taught as though Pentecost happened in 1776, and as though Franklin, Jefferson, and Washington were numbered among the apostles with Paine perhaps playing the role of Judas. But a Christian view of history and a Christianized version of history are two entirely different things.

Sorta Christian Academy has allowed itself, in the minds of some, to become "You're-Our-Last-Chance Christian School." Thus, Sorta receives hostile students who do not want to be there, and whose parents do not understand the purpose and function of parental authority in Christian education. Unfortunately, Sorta does not understand this purpose or function either. This is how the school has drifted

into becoming the local rescue mission on the skid row of
education choices. Because the school has forgotten its primary responsibility to act as servant to biblical parents, Sorta
finds itself adrift; the teachers are frustrated, the parents are
clueless, and the students are surly. Without a core group of
thoughtful and obedient parents, Sorta is condemned to a
usurpation which cannot work.

Sorta Christian Academy sees itself as a little sister of the
government schools not really grown up yet. So, hat in hand,
Sorta has asked some government-approved agency to come
in and accredit its program. But if the government's seal of
approval were all that valuable, there would not be a market
for private Christian schools in the first place. Nevertheless,
because there is no biblical vision at Sorta, success is consequently measured by money, enrollment, buildings, basketball programs, and other things not essential for true education. Sorta is well on the way to finding out that accredited
schools are, in principle, controlled schools—sitting in the
government's lap, and fed from a can.

No way can be found which will enable Christian schools
to teach children to think and live as Christians when those
running the school do not think and live as Christians. This
is the central flaw in the assumptions governing Sorta—somehow it is thought that if enough Christians gather together
and start a school, they should be able to muddle their way
through. But they cannot; the Lord Jesus is not the headmas-
ter.

A Vision for Recovery

We have thrown away much, and there is much we have to
recover. C.S. Lewis once commented,

> We have lived to see the second death of ancient learning.
> In our time something which was once the possession of
> all educated men has shrunk to being the technical accom-
> plishment of a few specialists . . . . If one were looking for

a man who could not read Virgil though his father could, he might be found more easily in the twentieth century than in the fifth.[2]

Several difficulties beset anyone who wants to talk seriously about a recovery of classical learning in the context of classical Protestant culture. This should not be surprising; rebuilding anything is usually far more difficult than starting from scratch.

The first problem is the obvious one. The reason we need to rebuild is that we do not understand our heritage. We need to rebuild because of what we have lost; we do not know how to rebuild because we have lost it. The resultant problem demands constant humility from all who seek a reformation in education. Returning to the culture of the Protestant West is not something we know how to do. We may discover, by the grace of God, how to begin—which is in a different category.

The second difficulty arises from this high level of cultural illiteracy which surrounds us and which afflicts the education reformers as well as everyone else. In the land of the blind, the man who knows he is blind does have an advantage. Because so few people really understand what is involved in classical learning, very little effort in the right direction will soon reward an individual with the mantle of an expert. The blind man who knows he is blind might come to confuse his knowing with seeing. To a certain extent this temptation is an inevitable result of the whole mess. Our society knows excellence in violinists, wide-receivers, highway construction, *etc.*, but we do not know excellence in *belles-lettres*, neither do we know the classical education underlying such excellence. Even our modern "highbrow" publishers churn out offscourings; reading an Oxford Press catalog is like hear-

[2] C. S. Lewis, The Quotable Lewis (Wheaton, IL: Tyndale House, 1989), p. 178.

ing the London Symphony Orchestra play the greatest hits of the Bee Gees.

Given this void, and the pervasive ignorance, the temptation is to set up shop as "classicists" who are all pipe and no Latin or Greek, all hat and no cattle, all bombast and no decent metaphors. But everyone who is involved in this task of cultural reconstruction must acknowledge that we are all nothing more than a band of ignorant but powerful Visigoths, standing around at the base of a great aquaduct, wondering how they did it. We might figure it out, but not today or tomorrow.

Those modern Christians who want to rebuild a culture through the education of their children and grandchildren must begin with a confession that the modern church has no cultural soul, and that our situation is desperate. As evangelical Protestants we squandered our cultural capital, we spent our heritage, over the course of a century and a half. In no way will we rediscover the immense fortune we threw away. We did not misplace it; we spent it on painted ladies in beer joints. It is gone; if we want it back, we will have to earn it again. Consequently, a true recovery of cultural soul will not be accomplished readily or easily. Pretending to have it is easy enough, and requesting "the classical curriculum" from some company for $49.95 is also relatively painless. It is also relatively worthless. We must come to see that cultural restoration will be the result of hard, covenantal faithfulness over the course of generations. Attempts at posturing and purchasing serve only to provide this intense effort with some comic relief.

The third problem is our great enemy, egalitarianism. This is the pervasive envy that will not even allow us to acknowledge our ignorance and begin the task of restoring learning, without some one sending up loud shouts of alarm. "Who do they think *they* are?"

As classical and Christian schools form around the country, one of the most frequent questions presented is, "Are you trying to be elitist?" In case anyone was wondering, the expected answer to all such questions is, "No, we want to be just like everybody else." If you want to be different, if you want to be better, then you and your school are a menace.

This egalitarian machine has been so effective that sensible discussion of these issues is virtually impossible. Of course, the biblical pattern of education excludes haughtiness, pride, arrogance, and all the rest of it. And, of course, this disclaimer was made necessary because of the inevitable slanders directed at any attempts to restore cultural soul, classical learning, Christian character, and nobility of mind. Unfortunately, many of the slanders come from within the church.

However, like it or not, true biblical education over time will always result in a division between those Christians who build their cultural endeavors on a biblical foundation and who will prosper under God's cultural blessing, and those Christians who do not, and who remain in the cultural ghetto typified by a modern Christian merchandise shop. We once built great cathedrals; now we throw gospel frisbees.

Nevertheless, we live in a time of tremendous opportunity and change. A few generations ago, the idea of universal government education was accepted by virtually everyone. Now, as this once proud system of socialist education is toppling, we hear—everywhere—the exciting hum of a free-market school system starting up. No longer is private education an alternative for just a few. In the years to come we will no doubt see free-market education replace the failed experiment of government schools. Because free-market alternatives are not mandated by someone in a central office somewhere, these alternatives can be quite different from one another. And quite honestly, some of them represent genuinely bad ideas—but we are still protected by the freedom of the market. In the long run, in a free market, poor ideas don't work. Parents, as consumers, realize that Johnny can't read, write, or think, and they vote with their tuition checks. Many of the other education alternatives in the private sector are good, but still quite different from one another.

To say that an education is not Christian is to say that it is deficient in essential respects. The existence, nature, and attributes of God are not a detail about the world which can be safely ignored. If a student never learns who Oecolampadius was, he may still receive a sound education. But if he never learns who God is, it can hardly be said that he has received an education at all. As Christians, we obviously must insist that Christian education should be for everyone. After all, Christ commanded us to disciple (educate) the nations in the light of His gospel and all His commandments. There is no way to separate the requirements of the Great Commission from the process of education—the instruction of the nations in the light of God's Word.

This is not the case with classical education. It is not desirable for us to try to make classical education universal for each and every student. At the same time, in another sense, classical education is for everyone. Not every family needs to have their children in a classical and Christian school. But our culture needs to have a significant number of her future leaders thoroughly educated in the heritage of the West. The goal of classical and Christian schools is, therefore, to assist parents who desire to bring up their children to be such leaders and thinkers, well-equipped and trained in the history and letters of western culture. As this happens, everyone will benefit.

We believe that classical and Christian education is an idea whose time has come. The small number of schools pursuing this vision now are merely a small cloud on the horizon, the size of a man's fist. If the Lord is merciful to us, our modern Ahabs may get more than a little wet.

A Call to Parents

The answer to our education crisis is for parents to recover their role as parents before the Lord, according to His Word alone. The biblical answer is to be found in parents assuming the responsibility which God has given to them, and only to them, for the education and upbringing of their children. The task was not given to the schools or daycare centers.

Three major considerations are involved. The first is for Christian parents to acknowledge in prayer and confession that God has placed the responsibility for these children with them. The second is to take all appropriate actions consistent with this repentance. This means pulling the children out of the government schools, as well as any private schools which act like government schools. And it means pulling them out yesterday. The government schools are in full-scale rebellion against God, and they are kept alive by means of the involvement of Christians. The third is the constant involvement of both parents in the lives of their children, teaching them from the Word of God on a daily basis. In the home, in the church, in the private Christian school, the parents are responsible to see to it that their children are educated in just the way the Bible requires.

Until the responsibility for the failure of American education is assumed by the parents, we will not see reform in education. When that biblical responsibility is assumed, we will be fortunate to witness the collapse of a century-long endeavor by the state to get parents to sell their children.

Suggested Reading List

First a word about this reading list. It is merely intended to get you started in reading on the general subject of classical and Christian education in a profitable way. In no way should the list be considered as exhaustive. But for the one who begins reading here seriously, the reading will lead to other books, which in turn will prove to be edifying. ACCS and the writers in this volume of course do not endorse everything found in these books, but nevertheless believe them to be of tremendous value as you undertake the establishment of a classical and Christian school.

- *The Bible*, preferably a formal equivalence translation with stylistic class (*e.g.*, NKJV, KJV).
- Augustine, *On Christian Doctrine*, Great Books of the Western World Series, vol. 18. Chicago: William Benton, 1952, pp. 621-698.
- John Milton, *Areopagitica and Of Education*. Northbrook, IL: AHM Publishing, 1951.
- R.L. Dabney, *On Secular Education*. Moscow, ID, Canon Press, 1989.
- Douglas Wilson, *Recovering the Lost Tools of Learning*. Wheaton, IL, Crossway, 1991.
- Dorothy Sayers, *The Lost Tools of Learning*. Included as an appendix in *Recovering the Lost Tools of Learning*.
- John Milton Gregory, *The Seven Laws of Teaching*. Grand Rapids: Baker, 1979.

• Rudolph Flesch, *Why Johnny Can't Read*. New York: Harper & Row, 1955.

• C.S. Lewis, *The Abolition of Man*. New York: Macmillan, 1947.

• J. Gresham Machen, *Education, Christianity, and the State*. Jefferson, MD: Trinity Foundation, 1987.

• Rousas Rushdoony, *The Messianic Character of American Education*. Nutley, NJ: Craig Press, 1979.

• Stephen Perks, *The Christian Philosophy of Education Explained*. Whitby, England: Avant Books, 1992.

• Charles Cochrane, *Christianity & Classical Culture*. Oxford, England: Oxford University Press. Out of print, so keep your eye peeled in used book stores.

• Augustine, *City of God*. New York: Image Books, 1958.

• Christopher Dawson, *Religion and the Rise of Western Culture*. New York: Image Books, 1957.

• John Calvin, *Institutes of the Christian Religion*. Grand Rapids: Eerdmans, 1989.

• Richard Weaver, *Ideas Have Consequences*. Chicago: University of Chicago Press, 1948.

• Wilson, Jones, Callihan, *Classical Education & the Home School*. Moscow, ID: Canon Press, 1995.

• J.C. Ryle, *Holiness*. Durham, England: Evangelical Press, 1995 [1879].

• Neil Postman, *Amusing Ourselves to Death*. New York: Penguin Books, 1985

• Herbert Schlossberg, *Idols for Destruction*. Wheaton, IL: Crossway, 1990

• David Wells, *No Place for Truth*. Grand Rapids: Eerdmans, 1993.

• Irving Copi, *Introduction to Logic*. New York: Macmillan, 1978.

• David Kelley, *The Art of Reasoning with Symbolic Logic*. New York: W.W. Norton & Co., 1990.

• Patrick Hurley, *A Concise Introduction to Logic*. Belmont, CA: Wadsworth Pub. Co., 1991.

• Bergmann, Moor, Nelson, *The Logic Book*. McGraw-Hill Pub. Co., 1990.

• Douglas Wilson, *Introductory Logic*. Moscow, ID: Canon Press, 1990.

• Jim Nance, *Intermediate Logic*. Moscow, ID: Canon Press, 1996.

• John Frame, *The Doctrine of the Knowledge of God*. Phillipsburg, NJ: Presbyterian and Reformed, 1987.

• Mortimer Adler, *How to Read a Book*. New York: Simon & Schuster, 1940.

• Homer, *The Iliad* and *Odyssey* Available in different editions.

• Virgil, *The Aeneid*. Available in different editons.

• Shakespeare, *Hamlet, Macbeth, Much Ado About Nothing*. Available in different editions.

• Gene Edward Veith, *Reading Between the Lines*. Wheaton, IL: Crossway, 1990

• Gene Edward Veith, *Postmodern Times*. Wheaton, IL: Crossway, 1994

• Gene Edward Veith, *State of the Arts*. Wheaton, IL: Crossway, 1991

• John Frame, *Apologetics to the Glory of God*. Phillipsburg, NJ: Presbyterian & Reformed, 1994.

• Aristotle, *Art of Rhetoric*. Available in different editions.

• Quintilian, *Institutio Oratoria*. Available in different editions.

• Cicero, *Ad Herennium*. Available in different editions. Traditionally ascribed to Cicero.